RUHL

in an hour

BY JAMES AL-SHAMMA

SUSAN C. MOORE, SERIES EDITOR

PLAYWRIGHTS in an hour
know the playwright, love the play
IN AN HOUR BOOKS • HANOVER, NEW HAMPSHIRE • INANHOURBOOKS.COM
AN IMPRINT OF SMITH AND KRAUS PUBLISHERS, INC • SMITHANDKRAUS.COM

With grateful thanks to Carl R. Mueller, whose fascinating introductions to his translations of the Greek and German playwrights provided inspiration for this series.

Published by In an Hour Books
an imprint of Smith and Kraus, Inc.
177 Lyme Road, Hanover, NH 03755
inanhourbooks.com SmithandKraus.com

Know the playwright, love the play.

In an Hour, In a Minute, and Theater IQ are registered trademarks of
In an Hour Books.

© 2009 by In an Hour Books
All rights reserved
Manufactured in the United States of America
First edition: April 2010
10 9 8 7 6 5 4 3 2 1

THE CLEAN HOUSE. © 2003, 2006 by Sarah Ruhl. Reprinted by permission of Theatre Communications Group. For performance rights, contact Samuel French, Inc. (www.samuelfrench.com) (212-206-8990).

DEAD MAN'S CELL PHONE. © 2008 by Sarah Ruhl. Reprinted by permission of Theatre Communications Group. For performance rights, contact Samuel French, Inc. (www.samuelfrench.com) (212-206-8990).

EURYDICE. © 2003, 2006 by Sarah Ruhl. Reprinted by permission of Theatre Communications Group. For performance rights, contact Samuel French, Inc. (www.samuelfrench.com) (212-206-8990).

IN THE NEXT ROOM (OR THE VIBRATOR PLAY). © 2009 by Sarah Ruhl. Reprinted by permission of Bruce Ostler, Bret Adams Ltd. For performance rights, contact Bruce Ostler (bostler@bretadamsltd.net)

LATE. © 2003, 2006 by Sarah Ruhl. Reprinted by permission of Theatre Communications Group. For performance rights, contact Bruce Ostler, Bret Adams Ltd. (bostler@bretadamsltd.net)

MELANCHOLY PLAY. © 2002, 2006 by Sarah Ruhl. Reprinted by permission of Theatre Communications Group. For performance rights, contact Bruce Ostler, Bret Adams Ltd. (bostler@bretadamsltd.net)

PASSION PLAY. © 2009 by Sarah Ruhl. Reprinted by permission of Bruce Ostler, Bret Adams Ltd. For performance rights, contact Bruce Ostler (bostler@bretadamsltd.net)

Front cover design by Dan Mehling, dmehling@gmail.com
Text design by Kate Mueller, Electric Dragon Productions
Book production by Dede Cummings Design, DCDesign@sover.net

ISBN-13: 978-1-936232-36-9
ISBN-10: 1-936232-36-7
Library of Congress Control Number: 2009943233

CONTENTS

Why Playwrights in an Hour?

This new series by Smith and Kraus Publishers titled Playwrights in an Hour has a dual purpose for being: one academic, the other general. For the general reader, this volume, as well as the many others in the series, offers in compact form the information needed for a basic understanding and appreciation of the works of each volume's featured playwright. Which is not to say that there don't exist volumes on end devoted to each playwright under consideration. But inasmuch as few are blessed with enough time to read the splendid scholarship that is available, a brief, highly focused accounting of the playwright's life and work is in order. The central feature of the series, a thirty- to forty-page essay, integrates the playwright into the context of his or her time and place. The volumes, though written to high standards of academic integrity, are accessible in style and approach to the general reader as well as to the student and, of course, to the theater professional and theatergoer. These books will serve for the brushing up of one's knowledge of a playwright's career, to the benefit of theater work or theatergoing. The Playwrights in an Hour series represents all periods of Western theater: Aeschylus to Shakespeare to Wedekind to Ibsen to Williams to Beckett, and on to the great contemporary playwrights who continue to offer joy and enlightenment to a grateful world.

Carl R. Mueller
School of Theater, Film and Television
Department of Theater
University of California, Los Angeles

Introduction

S till barely thirty-six, Sarah Ruhl has swiftly become one of the most frequently produced dramatists of our time. Not too long ago, when one would have been required to add the qualifier "female" dramatists, this would have been unimaginable. But there has been a large accumulation of plays by women in the last few decades, making sexual identification less important. Still, though progress has been made, women still experience prejudice in the theater world. For instance, the plays of female writers continue to be less produced than those of male writers.

Older people like myself, with longer memories than Ruhl's typical audience, remember a time when women playwrights were as scarce as male secretaries. After naming Susan Glaspell, one of Eugene O'Neill's contemporaries at the Provincetown Playhouse in the teens of the last century, and Sophie Treadwell (author of *Machinal*) in the twenties, and most notably Lillian Hellman, in the thirties, forties, fifties, and sixties, the list of significant women in the profession would have been exhausted. That all began to change with the advent of feminism in the sixties. Still, glass ceilings continue to block entry into some American professions, including, to some extent, the theater. But the presence of maturing female playwrights like Sarah Ruhl will hopefully shatter those ceilings. Indeed, one might ask if there would be an American drama today without Maria Irene Fornes, Lorraine Hansberry, Adrienne Kennedy, Paula Vogel, Beth Henley, Wendy Wasserstein, Marsha Norman, Suzan-Lori Parks, Tina Howe, Caryl Churchill, Lynn Nottage, Anna Deveare Smith, Rebecca Gilman, Theresa Rebeck, not to mention all those I have neglected to cite.

One of Paula Vogel's students in her celebrated playwriting program at Brown (Vogel now heads the department at the Yale School of

Drama), Sarah Ruhl has quickly become a mainstay of the resident theater movement, as well as Off-Broadway. She first became known to New York audiences with her comedy about immigrant women and middle-class wives, *The Clean House* in 2004, which is just one of the plays she has recently been producing at a remarkable rate — about one every year. Other productions include plays based on Greek mythological themes such as *Eurydice* and *Demeter in the City,* as well as plays inspired by other writers and forms, like *Orlando* and *Passion Play, a cycle.*

She attracted critical interest most recently with *In the Next Room (or the vibrator play),* a work that represents a considerable advance. While works like *The Clean House* are sometimes driven by a sitcom premise (a Brazilian woman who hates cleaning houses and allows the heroine's sister to do it, surreptitiously), or, like *Dead Man's Cell Phone,* which occasionally descends into excessive cuteness, *In the Next Room* shows real maturity in technique and subject matter. Set in the late nineteenth century, against the background of the invention of electricity, it is a study of the relationship between science and sensuality, or decorum and passion, as demonstrated through the attempt, by the heroine's doctor-husband, to cure hysteria by inducing orgasm. Inter-sexual and inter-racial like most of Ruhl's writing, the play employs a semi-detached, purposely naïve, vaguely surreal style to make important points about race, marriage, and sexual relations.

Ruhl is not afraid of taking on big subjects, and, young as she is, still has the time to cover a lot of ground. She is a playwright to be watched — bold, fearless, and intrepid.

Robert Brustein
Founding Director of the Yale and American Repertory Theatres
Distinguishing Scholar in Residence, Suffolk University
Senior Research Fellow, Harvard University

IN A MINUTE

AGE	DATE	
—	**1974**	**Enter Sarah Ruhl.**
1	1975	Edward Albee — *Seascape*
3	1977	Gordie Howe makes National Hockey League history by scoring 1,000th goal.
4	1978	Disco music and dancing take off.
5	1979	Pope John Paul II is the first pope to visit a communist country (Poland).
6	1980	Republicans take control of the Senate for first time since 1964.
7	1981	Ronald Reagan inaugurated as fortieth president of the U.S.
8	1982	Vietnam Veterans' War Memorial dedicated in Washington, D.C.
9	1983	M*A*S*H ends its 251-episode run.
10	1984	Harold Pinter — *One for the Road*
11	1985	Hole in the ozone layer discovered over Antarctica.
13	1987	Gorbachev announces policies of perestroika and glasnost.
17	1991	Tony Kushner — *Angels in America: A Gay Fantasia on National Themes, Part Two*
18	1992	*Silence of the Lambs* wins five Oscars.
19	1993	World Trade Center is bombed; seven die.
20	1994	O. J. Simpson's murder trial mesmerizes America.
21	1995	eBay revolutionizes online shopping.
22	1996	Rock and Roll Museum, designed by I. M. Pei, opens in Cleveland.
23	1997	Paula Vogel — *How I Learned to Drive*
24	**1998**	**Sarah Ruhl adapts *Orlando* by Virginia Woolf.**
25	1999	A 23,000-year-old frozen woolly mammoth is discovered in Siberia.
26	2000	J. K Rowling — *Harry Potter and the Goblet of Fire*
28	**2002**	**Sarah Ruhl — *Melancholy Play***
29	2003	Terrorists attack the UN headquarters in Baghdad.
30	**2004**	**Sarah Ruhl — *The Clean House***
31	**2005**	**Sarah Ruhl — *Passion Play, a cycle***
32	**2006**	**Sarah Ruhl — *Demeter in the City***
33	**2007**	**Sarah Ruhl — *Dead Man's Cell Phone***
34	2008	"Don't Stop the Music" by Rihanna tops the charts.
35	**2009**	**Sarah Ruhl — *In the Next Room (or the vibrator play)***

A snapshot of the playwright's world. From historical events to pop-culture and the literary landscape of the time, this brief list catalogues events that directly or indirectly impacted the playwright's writing. Play citations refer to premiere dates.

HER WORKS

DRAMA

Dog Play (reading)

Orlando (adapted from Virginia Woolf)

Anna Around the Neck (adapted from Anton Chekhov)

The Lady with the Lapdog (adapted from Anton Chekhov)

Virtual Meditation #1

Melancholy Play: a contemporary farce

Late: a cowboy song

Eurydice

The Clean House

Passion Play

Demeter in the City

Dead Man's Cell Phone

Passion Play, a cycle in three parts (revised)

Snowless

In the Next Room (or the vibrator play)

The Three Sisters (adapted from Anton Chekhov)

COLLECTIONS

Ruhl, Sarah. *The Clean House and Other Plays*. New York: Theatre Communications Group, 2006.

ESSAYS

Ruhl, Sarah. "Six Small Thoughts on Fornes, the Problem of Intention, and Willfulness." *Theatre Topics* 11, no. 2 (September 2001): 187–204.

This section presents a complete list of the playwright's works in chronological order.

———. "Sarah Ruhl, 'Dead Man's Cell Phone.'" Playwrights on Writing. *Los Angeles Times*, September 28, 2008. www.latimes.com/entertainment/news/arts/la-sarah-ruhl28-2008sep28,0,3028606.story.

———. "Essays I Don't Have Time to Write." *Device*, September–December 2008. http://device.papertheatre.org/.

———. "The Baltimore Waltz and the Plays of My Childhood." In *The Play That Changed My Life: America's Foremost Playwrights and the Plays That Influenced Them,* edited by Ben Hodges, 119–127. Milwaukee: Applause, 2009.

Onstage with Ruhl

Introducing Colleagues and
Contemporaries of Sarah Ruhl

 THEATER

Nilo Cruz, Cuban-American playwright
Beth Henley, American playwright
Tony Kushner, American playwright
Suzan-Lori Parks, American playwright
Sam Shepard, American playwright
Tom Stoppard, Czech-British playwright
Paula Vogel, American playwright
Les Waters, English director

 ARTS

Pina Bausch, German choreographer
Ray Charles, American singer and pianist
Christo and Jeanne-Claude, Bulgarian and French artists
Merce Cunningham, American dancer and choreographer
Plácido Domingo, Spanish tenor
Michael Jackson, American musician, dancer, and entertainer
Norah Jones, American vocalist
Wynton Marsalis, American jazz musician

 FILM

Halle Berry, American actor
Jane Campion, New Zealand director
Peter Jackson, New Zealand director
Sean Penn, American actor
Brad Pitt, American actor

This section lists contemporaries whom the playwright may or may not have known.

Martin Scorsese, American director
Steven Spielberg, American director and producer
Meryl Streep, American actor

POLITICS/MILITARY

Tony Blair, British prime minister
George W. Bush, American president
Bill Clinton, American president
Hillary Clinton, American first lady, senator, and secretary of state
Saddam Hussein, Iraqi dictator
Nelson Mandela, South African president
Barack Obama, American president
Ronald Reagan, American president

SCIENCE

Jacques Cousteau, French oceanographer
Francis Crick, English molecular biologist, physicist, and neuro-
    scientist
K. Eric Drexler, American engineer
Jerry Hall and Robert Stillman, American geneticists
Luc Montagnier, French immunologist
John Nash, American mathematician and economist
Claude Shannon, American mathematician
Norman Thagard, American astronaut

LITERATURE

Chinua Achebe, Nigerian novelist, poet, and critic
Italo Calvino, Italian novelist, short-story writer, and essayist
Anne Carson, Canadian poet and essayist
Gabriel García Márquez, Colombian novelist, short-story writer,
    essayist, and journalist
Alice McDermott, American novelist
V. S. Naipaul, West Indian novelist and essayist
Arundhati Roy, Indian novelist
Salman Rushdie, Indian-British novelist and essayist

RELIGION/PHILOSOPHY

Benedict XVI, German pope

Noam Chomsky, American philosopher and linguist

Dalai Lama, leader-in-exile of Tibetan Buddhism

Jacques Derrida, French philosopher

Jerry Falwell, American evangelist

Michel Foucault, French philosopher

John Paul II, Polish pope

Mother Teresa, Albanian Roman Catholic nun

SPORTS

Lance Armstrong, American cyclist

Florence Griffith-Joyner, American track and field athlete

Magic Johnson, American basketball player

Michael Jordan, American basketball player

Garry Kasparov, Russian chess player

Michael Phelps, American swimmer

Venus and Serena Williams, American tennis players

Zinedine Zidane, French soccer player

INDUSTRY/BUSINESS

Timothy Berners-Lee, English inventor

Michael Bloomberg, American businessman and New York City
    mayor

Michael Eisner, American CEO of Disney

David Geffen, American record executive, film producer, and
    theater producer

Alan Greenspan, Federal Reserve chairman

Steve Jobs, American cofounder of Apple

Rupert Murdoch, Australian media mogul

Craig Newmark, American founder of Craigslist

RUHL

in an hour

BAGGING MEDUSA'S HEAD

In *Six Memos for the Next Millennium*, Italo Calvino describes how Perseus conquers Medusa:

> The only hero able to cut off Medusa's head is Perseus, who flies with winged sandals; Perseus, who does not turn his gaze upon the face of the Gorgon but only upon her image reflected in his bronze shield. . . . To cut off Medusa's head without being turned to stone, Perseus supports himself on the very lightest of things, the winds and the clouds, and fixes his gaze upon what can be revealed only by indirect vision, an image caught in a mirror.

He is careful never to look at the bagged head and employs it as a weapon, turning its ossifying stare against his enemies. His strength "always lies in a refusal to look directly, but not in a refusal of the reality in which he is fated to live; he carries the reality with him and accepts it as his particular burden."

This is the core of the book. The essay places the playwright in the context of his or her world and analyzes the influences and inspirations within that world.

Like Perseus, Sarah Ruhl carries a particular burden, that of the loss of her father to cancer when she was twenty, and also like the Greek hero, she handles it with lightness. Heavy issues of life, love, and death lie at the heart of her drama, but she treats them with a deft touch, keeping humor close at hand even when plumbing the depths of despair and bereavement. Ruhl admires Calvino's *Memos*, specifically his first chapter, titled "Lightness." She explains in an interview with John Lahr, "Lightness isn't stupidity. . . . It's actually a philosophical and aesthetic viewpoint, deeply serious, and has a kind of wisdom — stepping back to be able to laugh at horrible things even as you're experiencing them."

Ruhl's voice is unique in American theater. Her nonrealistic, highly theatrical style aligns her with Thornton Wilder, John Guare, and Tony Kushner. She has worked through her grief across a number of plays, and an appreciation of the ephemeral informs her writing. If one were forced to summarize her aesthetic in two words, *grief* and *whimsy* would serve, reflecting as they do the application of lightness to heaviness and darkness. What is unique about Ruhl is this light touch, expressed through fantasy and magic realism and informed by a poetic sensibility and erudite intelligence. Although only in her mid-thirties, Ruhl has already received widespread recognition and commendation. Most noteworthy is her status as a Pulitzer finalist and a MacArthur Fellowship recipient. She is presently one of the most-produced female playwrights in the United States.

Ruhl began to charm the snakes on Medusa's head as early as two months after her father's death, as an undergraduate in a playwriting class conducted by Paula Vogel at Brown University. Vogel's esteem for her student cannot be overstated. Quoted in an article by Celia Wren, Vogel claims that her "most significant contribution to the American theatre" has been to encourage Ruhl's playwriting. Vogel is, herself, an accomplished playwright, counting among her accolades a Pulitzer Prize for perhaps her best-known work, *How I Learned to Drive*. During her tenure as director of the playwriting program at

Brown University, Vogel mentored numerous young talents including Nilo Cruz, who went on to win his own Pulitzer Prize. In an article by Kerry Reid, she explains, "There has not been another Sarah. I've taught at Brown for 20 years and I've had many extraordinary writers. I'm lucky I got to experience one Sarah Ruhl in my life and I know that." (Vogel since left Brown University for a five-year appointment as chair of the playwriting department at Yale School of Drama beginning July 1, 2008.) In an article in *Bomb*, she predicts that Ruhl is "going to become her own vocabulary word" and describes the moment at which she first recognized her student's immense talent:

> [Ruhl] came into my intensive advanced playwriting seminar some 15 years ago. A sophomore, but I thought at first she was a senior: she was quiet and serious, but so obviously possessed a mind that came at aesthetics from a unique angle. I assigned an exercise: to write a short play with a dog as protagonist. Sarah Ruhl wrote of her father's death from that unique angle: a dog is waiting by the door, waiting for the family to come home, unaware that the family is at his master's funeral, unaware of the concept of death.
>
> And, oh yes, the play was written with Kabuki stage techniques, in gorgeous, emotionally vivid language. I sat with this short play on my lap in my study, and sobbed.

When Ruhl later approached Vogel with the idea of writing her thesis on "the representation of the actress in the nineteenth-century novel," unsurprisingly Vogel insisted on a play instead.

The writing exercise described by Vogel gives an early indication of Ruhl's style and thematic concerns. Composed only a few months after her father's passing, it introduces the themes of death and bereavement that would continue to absorb Ruhl for years to come. It demonstrates her ability to elicit a strong emotional response, and the element of fantasy, initiated through the assigned canine protagonist, is advanced through inclusion of elements from Kabuki theater. Ruhl's poetic sensibility is on display as well, alluded to in Vogel's description of her "emotionally vivid language." Indeed, Ruhl wrote poems before she wrote plays, publishing a collection of verse, "Death in Another Country," at age twenty. The collection was bundled with the work of two other poets in a volume titled *Troika VI*, published by Thorntree Press in 1995; it is now out of print. In an interview with Caridad Svitch (herself a noted playwright), Ruhl draws parallels between these two modalities:

> Poetry and plays, in a very obvious way, have this in common: There is more white space in their margins than there is print. What's filling up all that space? Song, stillness, speculation — all kinds of invisible things. Of course, a good fiction writer doesn't fill in the gaps, but you have to know when to keep your mouth shut to be a poet or to be a playwright. You have to know when to keep your mouth shut so that the lines are in fact lines rather than paragraphs, so that the line can sing.

Ruhl carefully crafts every line and delights in surprising juxtapositions. Richard Corley, who directed *Eurydice* at Madison Repertory Theatre, is quoted in the Wren article: "Sarah Ruhl has a reason (and a vision) for every line, . . . and my advice to directors is: Pay attention. Beneath that lovely, generous exterior is a fierce intelligence, which we ignore at our peril." Wren concisely summarizes Ruhl's style:

> While diverse on the level of story, the plays share certain traits: a steely lyricism; a pronounced whimsy; a deceptive spareness, masking an almost metaphysical intensity; and a quirky, compassionate humor that often coexists with deep sadness.

In the same article, Les Waters, who directed three productions of *Eurydice* and the world premiere of *In the Next Room (or the vibrator play)*, praises her aptitude for advancing plot with lyrical dialogue: "She's one of the few people I know who can write a form of dialogue that's poetic, where the poetry is welded to the action."

In addition to Vogel, Ruhl has studied playwriting with Mac Wellman, Nilo Cruz, and Maria Irene Fornes. The influence of Fornes is evident in Ruhl's essay "Six Small Thoughts on Fornes, the Problem of Intention, and Willfulness," published in 2001. In it, Ruhl examines the concepts of intention and will in current theatrical practice. Ruhl sides with Fornes, who questions the prevalent Stanislavskian insistence on character objectives. Both legitimize the depiction of emotional states of being in the absence of willfulness and protest a psychological realism in which action and emotion are traced exclusively through cause and effect. In the interview with Lahr, Ruhl expresses a preference for a type of drama based on Ovid rather than Aristotle, one abounding in small transformations rather than one in which "a person wants something, comes close to getting it but is smashed down, then finally gets it, or not, then learns something from the experience." This does not mean that Ruhl's plays are plotless. She does leave space, however, for small transformations and unprovoked emotional states. As Svich notes, Ruhl's characters "are in the 'real' world but also live in a more suspended state."

HER LIFE

Born on January 24, 1974, Ruhl grew up in the Chicago suburb of Wilmette and also spent considerable time visiting her family's home state of Iowa. As Ruhl was growing up, her mother, Kathy Kehoe Ruhl, acted in and directed plays while teaching high school English; she now holds a Ph.D. in language, literacy, and rhetoric from the University of Illinois. Ruhl's late father, Patrick, marketed toys for a number of years. As noted in the Lahr article, he loved "puns, reading, language, and jazz" and, according to his daughter, "should have been a history professor." Her older sister, Kate, is a psychiatrist.

Ruhl began telling stories at an early age, stating in "A Conversation" in *Lincoln Center Theater* that "my mother claims that before I could write, I would dictate stories to her and she would write them down." In an interview with Peter Gianopulos, she says that the first story she wrote was about "a wedding between two vegetables who lived on different sides of the refrigerator." Ruhl describes her early career ambitions and her first play in the Svich interview:

> In first grade, I thought that when I grew up I would write stories and be a teacher. . . . In fourth grade, I briefly entertained the idea that I would own a restaurant. I thought it would be the perfect use of all my skills: I could write a description of the food on the menu, and I could also draw pictures on the menu. I'm not sure when I realized that there was more to being a restaurateur than making menus. I did write a courtroom drama involving landmasses, in the fourth grade. There was a disagreement between an isthmus and an island, and the sun had to come down and settle the matter in the end. My teacher Mr. Spangenberger refused to put it on. . . . I didn't suspect that I would be a playwright from a young age.

As she relates in the National Public Radio profile "Playwright Sarah Ruhl Entertains with Big Ideas," the topic of her first play demonstrates both her sense of whimsy and her love of language: "I loved the words like 'isthmus' and 'peninsula.'"

Ruhl spent time in the theater from an early age. When she was five years old, her mother took her to rehearsals at which Ruhl would take notes. She told Dinitia Smith, "I would think they hadn't gotten it quite right." She started taking classes at the Piven Theatre Workshop while in the fourth grade. Located in Evanston, Illinois, and founded over thirty-five years ago by Joyce Piven and her late husband, Byrne Piven, the workshop boasts such alumni as John and Joan Cusack, Jeremy Piven, Aidan Quinn, Lili Taylor, Harry Lennix, Kate Walsh, Hope Davis, and Polly Noonan, who has appeared in many of Ruhl's plays. The Pivens founded the workshop to continue the improvisational work of Viola Spolin. In the Lahr article, Joyce Piven identifies source materials: "We acted stories, myths, fairy tales, folk tales, and literary tales — Chekhov, Eudora Welty, Flannery O'Connor, Salinger." The emphasis was on language, not scenery, and on transformation: The theater "didn't use props, and didn't have sets. Language did everything. So, from an early age: no fourth wall, and things can transform in the moment." Ruhl claims, in the Reid interview, that this early training helped shape her playwriting aesthetic:

> I think there's something specific about the training of the Piven workshop that comes into my work. . . . It's an emphasis on transformation and discovery over and above a dramaturgy of Aristotelian conflict. There's respect for language and the melody of a line that Joyce and Byrne [Piven] instill in actors, rather than having a mannered or shaggy subtext. The playfulness they encourage comes into my work. You just can't help but take in a respect for organic playfulness when you come through the workshop.

In the same article, Jessica Thebus, who directed *The Clean House* at the Goodman Theatre and *Melancholy Play* at the Piven Workshop, agrees with Ruhl's assessment:

> *Melancholy Play* was the first full-length play of [Ruhl's] that I read. I thought I saw the structures of improvisation and theatre games and long-form within the play in a way that is hard to explain. I feel like the people in her plays are improvising together in a dynamic that is very familiar to me.

The workshop was also involved in the development of *The Clean House*, staging its first sit-down reading and three performances as a workshop presentation, and it commissioned and premiered *Orlando*, Ruhl's adaptation of the Virginia Woolf novel, as well as her adaptations of Chekhov's short stories.

When Ruhl was twenty, in August 1994, her father died of cancer (a submandibular salivary gland tumor that metastasized to the bones) after fighting the disease for two years, an event that would have a profound impact on her and her art. She graduated from Brown University in Providence, Rhode Island, with a B.A. in English in 1997; her undergraduate work included a year spent studying English literature at Pembroke College in Oxford. She worked a variety of jobs for the next two years, including teaching arts education in public schools, before returning to Brown for an M.F.A. in playwriting, which she completed in 2001. After graduating, she lived in New York, Chicago, and Los Angeles, eventually returning to New York City, where she now resides in Manhattan. With Paula Vogel and Anne Fausto-Sterling officiating, she and Anthony Charuvastra, now a child psychiatrist, were married on a mountaintop outside Los Angeles in 2005 after a seven-year courtship. Ruhl gave birth to their daughter Anna in spring 2006.

EURYDICE

In an examination of Ruhl's plays, a good place to start is *Eurydice*, a powerful study of bereavement that premiered at Madison Repertory Theatre in September 2003 under the direction of Richard Corley. Time and again, it has wrung strong emotion, and even tears, from even that most obdurate of theatergoers, the critic. In *The Boston Globe*, Louise Kennedy details a particularly strong and intimately personal response:

> It's a fascinating night in the theater, and I scribble excited notes for the review I plan to write the next day. There's a lot to think about, a lot to write about, and that fills me with energy and delight.
>
> Then it's over, and I walk to my car. I get in, put the key in the ignition, and break down into heaving, wracking sobs. All I can think about is the image of Eurydice's father. . . .

I saw this play on Oct. 3; my father had died Sept. 7. Ours was a complicated relationship — whose isn't? — and though I had gone through the rituals of mourning I have been troubled by finding myself unable to cry more than about five tears at a time.

But now, picturing this imaginary father spinning a web of love around his imaginary child, I feel all the sorrow and guilt and confusion and anger and loss that I have been refusing to let in. I cry for a long time. And then, feeling just as cleansed and purified and exhausted as we were promised by all those theories of catharsis in freshman English, I drive the two hours back home. . . . [T]his play, more than most I have seen this year, continues to haunt me.

She speculates that the play's impact may owe something to the public mourning for strangers that followed the collapse of the World Trade Center and the ensuing struggle between "remembering and forgetting, between turning back and moving on."

In the Greek myth, Eurydice dies of a snakebite on her wedding day. Her grief-stricken groom, Orpheus, descends to the underworld, where, moved by his exquisite, musical lamentation, Hades and his wife, Persephone allow him to retrieve his bride. They prohibit him, however, from glancing back at her on the way out; the urge, of course, proves irresistible, and Eurydice is whisked back to the underworld. Ruhl claims to have written the play to have one last conversation with her deceased father. In most retellings, Orpheus is the protagonist. Ruhl, however, places Eurydice center stage and introduces the figure of her father in the underworld. The stories that Eurydice's father tells are, indeed, taken verbatim from tapes that Ruhl recorded of her own father when he was ill with cancer. By the time Orpheus arrives to retrieve her, an empowered Eurydice has decided that she would prefer to stay with her father and deliberately sabotages her husband by calling out his name and compelling him to look at her. Ruhl has faithfully captured the process of bereavement from her own experience, and much of the impact of the play derives from watching the young couple traverse the landscape of mourning. Even though the play ends in grief-filled silence, Ruhl's trademark whimsy and poetic turn of phrase are evident throughout. A chorus of three stones greets Eurydice upon her arrival in the underworld, and the Lord of the Underworld grows from a tot on a tricycle to a ten-foot-tall man.

A duality served as the grain of sand to Ruhl's pearl, as quoted in the interview with Svich:

> I began to work on *Eurydice* with one image in mind: Eurydice follows Orpheus, then she calls his name, which startles him, and he turns around. This image — of language taking over music — continued to circulate, and around that image, the play sprang up.

Thematically, Ruhl has configured a sequence of dualities that includes music/language, life/death, romantic love/paternal love, overworld/ underworld, lightness/heaviness, farmer/artist, memory/forgetfulness, child/adult, father/husband, high/low, internal/external, and art/nature. The final synthesis of most of these equals death.

The play overflows with references to water — in the dialogue, sound effects, and set pieces, which include "rusty exposed pipes," a water pump, and "an abstracted River of Forgetfulness." In his design for all three Les Waters productions, Scott Bradley extended the metaphor by pumping the elevator full of one hundred gallons of water that flood the stage when the door slides open. As documented in "Production Notebook" in *American Theatre*, Bradley based his design on "turn-of-the-century baths and swimming pools," giving the set the appearance of the bottom of a Victorian-era swimming pool; water drips down the walls to complete the effect.

Water is frequently associated with grieving in the play. In Orpheus' dream, the water coming out of Eurydice's hair suggests a torrential outpouring of sorrow and the salty lake into which they fall, a pool of tears. Eurydice is drawn to water: She leaves her wedding twice for the water pump, she asks the Nasty Interesting Man for a glass of water, and she requests a bath when she arrives in the underworld. As water is associated with tears and bereavement, her craving for it manifests a compulsion to attend to the unfinished business of mourning for her father. It is only after he has dipped himself in the river and lies still on the floor that finally, like a saturated cloud, she releases her watery load.

Ruhl associates water not only with grieving but also with forgetfulness. Among the several rivers in the classical Greek underworld are the River Styx, across which the boatman Charon ferries the deceased into Hades, and the River Lethe, which the newly deceased must drink from to erase all memory of their previous lives. Ruhl's stage directions call for the inclusion of the River Lethe as "an abstracted River of Forgetfulness" in which both Eurydice and the Father both dip themselves as they seek oblivion. The hand-operated water pump from the First Movement doubled as this river in the Les Waters productions. The raining elevator combines the functionality of both rivers, providing passage and erasing memory. Through its association with both the River Styx and grief, water links the transition from life into death with the process of bereavement.

THE CLEAN HOUSE

Whereas *Eurydice* carries the full weight of a daughter's sorrow, Ruhl approaches death with a lighter touch in *The Clean House*. She employs magic realist techniques that heighten the sense of whimsy and concludes the latter in hopeful mirth rather than devastating silence. In a world in which jokes can kill, Matilde euthanizes the terminally ill Ana, then recalls the comical circumstances of her own birth and envisions heaven as a place where "everyone is laughing." Death pushes characters apart in *Eurydice*. Even though it initially delivers Eurydice to her father, it tears her away from Orpheus and ultimately isolates each of them. By contrast, in *The Clean House* it draws together a nurturing community of women around the ailing Ana. Although the play contains its share of grief, the final effect is one of lightness and release. As a playwright, in terms of bereavement, Ruhl has advanced from the stage of despair into that of adjustment and even acceptance.

In *The Clean House*, a young woman, Matilde (pronounced "Ma-chil-gee"), has immigrated from Brazil to the United States after her parents died and is working as a live-in housekeeper to married doctors, Lane and Charles. Unfortunately, Matilde hates to clean. Unbeknownst to Lane, her sister, Virginia, comes to Matilde's aid and cleans the house. In the meantime, Charles has fallen in love with a patient, Ana, on whom he has performed a mastectomy. Charles and Ana come to Lane's house, asking for forgiveness while claiming that they are faultless since they have discovered each other as soul mates. At approximately the same time, Lane discovers that her sister has been cleaning her house and threatens to fire Matilde. When Ana hears about this, she offers Matilde a job; Lane resists, and as a result, Matilde ends up splitting her time between the two households. When Ana's cancer recurs, she refuses further medical treatment. Charles flies off to Alaska in search of a natural, plant-based remedy, leaving the women to nurse Ana.

Matilde's parents continually amused one another and were, she claims, "the funniest people in Brazil." Indeed, the last joke her father told her mother was so funny that it killed her; he committed suicide soon after. Ruhl stipulates that the actors playing Charles and Ana should double as Matilde's parents, who appear in flashbacks. When Matilde thinks up the perfect and fatal joke, she honors Ana's request to perform euthanasia on her. In the stage directions, Ruhl describes Matilde's journey as one "from the dead to the living and back again." Matilde wears black to signify that she is in mourning, and her search for, and implementation of, the perfect, deadly joke signifies bereavement and succession. Through character doubling, Matilde symbolically rectifies her mother's murder as an act of mercy rather than an accident. Matilde acquires and puts to proper use the power that her father possessed but was unable to control. The perfect joke thus functions as an incantation might in a shamanic ritual, as a means of gathering and focusing otherworldly power.

Ruhl employs a variety of magic realist techniques such as the literalization of metaphor, mirroring, the metaphorization of space, the normalization of the fantastic, and the employment of an impartial narrator-figure. As a literary term, *magic realism* was first applied in the middle of the twentieth century to South American authors who wrote from a presumably magical continent. As a postcolonial strategy, the magical in magic realism challenges European rationalism, offering up an alternative and equally legitimate worldview. Like the magic realist, the shaman travels from the ordinary to the fantastic and back again, experiencing both ordinary life and a magical realm of spirits. Shamanism connects the visible to the invisible, the real to the magical, logos to mythos. The magic realist style of the play supports a shamanistic interpretation of Matilde's joke.

An overheard conversation provided the idea for *The Clean House*. Attending a party for doctors with her husband, who is himself a psychiatrist, Ruhl overheard a woman complaining that her Brazilian maid refused to clean, even after she had had her medicated. In an interview with Wendy Weckwerth, Ruhl reveals her approach as inspired by the anecdote:

> Here's this woman who thinks she's transcended cleaning because of her education. It's as though liberal-minded career women are too good to clean their own house. That fascinates me on a political level, but also on spiritual and psychological levels. What does it mean to be alienated from your own dirt? What does it mean for the upper classes to be alienated from the exigencies of everyday living, so that they're not noticing what accumulates over time? When I first started the play I was mostly interested in the pure politics of it — this woman I met at the cocktail party made me

so angry. Then I realized she had to become more human to me if I was going to write about her.

The overheard statement became the opening monologue of the play, following Matilde's joke. The shift in Ruhl's concern from the political to the personal manifests in the course taken by the play, which begins with the provocative monologue but then quickly moves into an examination of the relationships between four women. Although they are from varying socioeconomic backgrounds, ultimately their similarities overcome their differences.

As in *Eurydice*, Ruhl's family history figures significantly in *The Clean House*. Ruhl eulogizes her father in the former. In the latter, Ana's struggle resembles that of her father, who succumbed to cancer after a two-year battle. Breast cancer proved fatal to both the playwright's grandmothers, as it does to Ana. In the Pressley interview, Ruhl credits the sense of humor in the play to her father: "It's very much about my dad, in a way. . . . His sense of humor as he went through it. And humor being a kind of a saving grace." The sibling rivalry between Lane and Virginia may be traced to that between Ruhl and her older sister, Kate. The play is dedicated to her husband, Tony, and her sister, both of whom are doctors, as are uncles and a grandfather.

Ruhl was awarded the 2003–04 Susan Smith Blackburn Prize for *The Clean House*, and the play was also a 2005 Pulitzer Prize finalist. The first act was commissioned by the McCarter Theatre Center in Princeton, New Jersey, in 2000. In its full-length form, it premiered in September 2004 at Yale Repertory Theatre under the direction of Bill Rauch. It has been a regional theater favorite, during the 2005–06 season alone appearing in at least ten venues, including seven productions in the United States, four in Canada, and one in England. It finally landed in the Mitzi Newhouse Theatre at Lincoln Center for its New York premiere in October 2006. According to Ruhl, its relatively late appearance in New York was due not to a lack of interest, but rather to insufficient stage height: Of the theaters that approached her, only Lincoln Center could accommodate the balcony so crucial to the play's second act, and that venue was booked two years in advance.

MELANCHOLY PLAY

As in *Eurydice*, water imagery in *Melancholy Play: a contemporary farce* is frequently associated with sadness or, more precisely, the feeling of melancholy. A sudden rainfall prompts Tilly, the protagonist, to mourn the impermanence of flowers, and she later likens herself to a river of sorrow; characters longingly smell the ocean all the way from Illinois and dream of sea voyages; and drinking from a vial of tears transforms each of them into an almond. The object of loss here, however, is concealed, and the cause of Tilly's melancholy remains uncertain; she seems to enjoy the emotion for its own sake. In spite of this apparent vagueness, *Melancholy Play* may be read as a continued expression of the playwright's grief as manifested in the other two works, both through its celebration of melancholy and through explicit and implicit references to death. Indeed, the central crisis of the work, that of being transformed into an almond, serves as a metaphor for death, and the ever-present Julian, the cellist, functions as a death figure providing accompaniment as the ensemble partakes in a sort of Dance of Death as they progress toward the terminal "almond state."

Ruhl draws on Jacobean literature for inspiration, both in terms of dramatic presentation and style and for a definition of melancholy. She both directly quotes and paraphrases Richard Burton's *The Anatomy of Melancholy*, a seventeenth-century treatise that delves into the causes and cures of the malady in great detail. She insists that "Melancholy in this play is Bold, Outward, Sassy, Sexy and Unashamed. It is not introverted. It uses, instead, the language of Jacobean direct address." Ruhl explains further in her interview with Weckwerth:

> I was worried that it would be played as a meditation when I was looking for something more outward. That's why I refer

to Jacobean plays. In the plays of the Elizabethan and Jacobean periods melancholy is still an outward, yearning, active thing. It's not a depressive, internal, shaggy, filmic state. Even Hamlet's melancholy is just partially internalized; it's still very outward. When I started doing readings of the play I realized that many people of my generation don't think of melancholy in that Jacobean — or even 1940s-movies — way, where it can be an externalized longing.

The Black Death was a terrifying threat before, during, and after the reign of James I, and Ruhl has implanted references to this as well that collectively equate melancholy with the plague.

The play was first produced by the Piven Theatre in Evanston, Illinois, in June 2002, directed by Jessica Thebus. As Ken Prestininzi, who directed a later production at Brown University in November 2007, points out in Gray's preview in *The Providence Journal*, the word *play* in the title refers both to a theatrical work and an enjoyable engagement with something. Thus the title in conjunction with the subtitle, *a contemporary farce*, presents the dual contradictions of playing with melancholy and a melancholic farce. Ruhl plays with melancholy as she draws on the term's historical usage and contrasts it to the modern American notion of depression as an ailment that is best treated, and eradicated, through the application of pharmaceuticals. Each of the other characters falls in love, in turn, with Tilly because they find her sorrowful mood irresistible. She herself relishes the feeling and creates rich associations with the word *melancholy* through her invocation of foreign words that denote different types of sadness.

The work is a contemporary, as opposed to a traditional, farce for a number of reasons. The dictionary defines farce as "a light, humorous play in which the plot depends upon a skillfully exploited situation rather than upon the development of character." Ruhl certainly exploits the situation of Tilly's emotional state in a humorous fashion, but adds weight by giving serious consideration to that state. For example, the dolorous musical score performed on the cello lends a certain aura of gravitas. The subgenre to which the work most closely belongs would be the bedroom farce, which derives much of its situational humor from acts of infidelity. Although Tilly changes sexual partners several times during the play, these shifts fail to evoke the standard sense of moral transgression because none of the relationships are bounded by marriage. As a result, *Melancholy Play* is devoid of the subterfuge and evasion that provides the foundation for much of the comedy in a traditional bedroom farce.

The farcical plot can best be traced through Tilly's changing partnerships or, more generally, the attractive pull that her melancholy exerts on those she encounters. Her psychiatrist, Lorenzo the Unfeeling, falls for her first; she resists his advances, finding him altogether too cheerful. She develops a closer affinity for her tailor, Frank, who is somewhat melancholic himself. Next, a haircut leads to an intimate encounter with her stylist, Frances. However, that too is short-lived, as she becomes involved with an offstage character, a woman who writes obituaries. Along the way, Frances' live-in girlfriend, Joan, a nurse, also develops a crush on Tilly, although her love is not consummated. Midway through the play, the protagonist suddenly becomes inexplicably and relentlessly happy, and the rest of the characters, who had fallen in love with her due to her exquisite sadness, now find her intolerable. Frances meanwhile seems to have caught Tilly's melancholy and begins to change into an almond, completing the transformation when she downs a vial of Tilly's tears. Unable to change her back, the rest of the ensemble joins her in the "almond state" by partaking in a tear-drinking ceremony. To complete the farce, Frank and Frances discover that they are long-lost twins, separated at birth.

DEAD MAN'S CELL PHONE

As in *Eurydice* and *The Clean House*, Ruhl explores the themes of memory and death in *Dead Man's Cell Phone*. In *Eurydice*, memory serves as the very fabric of relationship and personality; in *The Clean House*, as the connective tissue binding the individual to the family of origin; and in *Dead Man's Cell Phone*, as a malleable, imaginary construct. The father revives Eurydice's personality by restoring language and memory, and Matilde conjures the ghosts of her parents through the act of remembering them. In *Dead Man's Cell Phone*, Jean fabricates stories about the deceased Gordon that recast him in a better light; in doing so, she constructs a fulfilled image of him for the benefit of his family and loved ones.

The plot revolves around Gordon's cell phone, which Jean acquires after discovering him dead of a heart attack in a café. Although a stranger to him, as the first to find him she feels compelled to notify his callers that he has passed away. In doing so, she becomes involved with the primary figures in his life, which include his mother, his wife, his brother, and his mistress. Jean, a lonely yet kind person, falls in love with the romantic image she constructs of Gordon — an image that is at odds with what she learns about him from his family and mistress. She ameliorates the suffering of Gordon's survivors by misleading each into believing he or she was foremost in his final thoughts. Jean travels to South Africa to handle some of Gordon's unfinished business. There she is seemingly killed and then transported to a peculiar afterlife in which souls are condemned to spend the rest of eternity with the person they loved the most. This person turns out to be Gordon, who quickly disillusions her. As the plot speeds toward its conclusion, she returns to the land of the living, where she is reunited with Gordon's brother, Dwight, with whom she realizes she has fallen in love. Upon learning of the nature of the afterlife from Jean, Gordon's mother throws herself on the barbecue and self-incinerates to be reunited with her eldest son. The play closes with Jean and Dwight pledging to love each other with "the strongest love in the world."

As Ruhl progresses in her plays farther and farther from the point of loss, the characterization of the deceased male resembles her own father less and less. The father in *Eurydice* is closely based on Ruhl's own; Matilde's father in *The Clean House* shares a strong sense of humor with Ruhl's father, although this characteristic is taken to a magic realist extreme. In *Dead Man's Cell Phone*, Gordon does not even fill the role of father but rather that of a love interest, albeit older. His selfishness and ruthlessness contrast sharply with the caring and concern displayed by Eurydice's and, by extension, Ruhl's own father. As the personality of the deceased changes, so does the relationship between the female protagonist and the deceased, which is nevertheless always marked by longing. This longing finds temporary fulfillment in Eurydice's reunion with her father, and is manifested and eventually released by Matilde through the visions of her parents, but is repudiated in Jean's encounter with Gordon. The afterworld that he inhabits bears no resemblance to the joyous heaven described by Matilde and is potentially even more unpleasant than the Greek-inspired underworld of *Eurydice*, which, although flat and gray, is also peaceful and quiet. The afterworld of *Dead Man's Cell Phone* traps one for eternity with the person one loved most, with all the potential psychological distress that this entails. Jean quickly finds Gordon to be intolerable; it is her good fortune that she is able to return to the land of the living.

Rebecca Bayla Taichman directed the premiere at Woolly Mammoth Theatre Company in Washington, D.C., in June 2007. Ruhl made slight revisions for productions in New York and Chicago in March 2008. The New York premiere occurred at Playwrights Horizons, featured Mary-Louise Parker as Jean, and was directed by Anne Bogart.

LATE: A COWBOY SONG

Late: a cowboy song premiered at the Ohio Theatre in New York City, produced by Clubbed Thumb, in April 2003 under the direction of Debbie Saivetz. The play features a love triangle with a lesbian twist and gender complications. At the conclusion, Mary leaves her abusive husband, Crick, for the other woman, Red, whose character description reads, "She's no cowgirl, she's a cowboy." Ruhl references *It's a Wonderful Life*, a 1946 film in which everyman George Bailey, played by Jimmy Stewart, sacrifices his dreams for the greater good, as Crick views the film on television on several occasions. Further, Mary in the play appears to be named after the movie wife. In the film, George abandons his plans to attend college, travel, and then "build things," instead rescuing his deceased father's savings and loan, marrying, and starting a family. The movie idealizes the American family as exemplified by that of George and Mary, which survives George's crisis of confidence and becomes stronger than ever.

Whereas George abandons his personal goals for the greater good, reluctantly at first but finally willingly, Ruhl's Crick focuses primarily on his own needs, behaves abusively toward his wife, and fails to redeem himself. In her book on domestic violence, Dawn Bradley Berry outlines three stages: (1) tension builds as the man becomes "edgy, critical, [and] irritable" while the woman appeases him; (2) the violent outburst; and (3) loving contrition, during which the man might apologize and ask for forgiveness, swearing to reform himself. The woman, grateful for her partner's positive behavior, willingly forgives the abuse, and the couple reconciles. The violence is liable to become more severe with each repetition, and the abuse may be physical, psychological, or both.

Crick cycles through this pattern. He is given to outbursts of anger and threatening behavior, which ultimately escalate to the point of physical violence. He throws a pot, a loaf of bread, and a Christmas present against the wall, makes his hand into a fist while arguing, and waits at home with a baseball bat in hand. During his final encounter with Mary, he "puts his hands on the back of her neck, hard." He and his wife typically reconcile through physical affection. As in the movie, the couple has been acquainted since childhood and experiences financial difficulties. Unlike George, however, Crick is unable to provide any semblance of economic stability.

Ruhl sets the myth of the American cowboy against that of the American family. Red personifies the rugged individual in opposition to the self-sacrificing family man. Ruhl's inclusion of the Marlboro Man in her setting evokes the mythos of the masculine. Ruhl alters the gender of this mythos by describing Red as a female cowboy. She is presumably anatomically female, although sexual ambiguity is not ruled out. Blue's androgyny and Red's masculinity challenge the hetero-normal relationship between Crick and Mary and, by extension, the idealized American family as depicted in *It's a Wonderful Life*. Indeed, Mary ultimately leaves her husband for the female cowboy.

Crick and Mary's baby, Blue, is born with both male and female sexual features. Mary expresses concern about the surgical procedure performed on her child: "I guess it's a girl now. I don't know why they couldn't have left well enough alone." Crick and Mary's tussle over the baby's name extends the battle over her identity. Crick prefers Jill because "things are going to be weird enough, without her having a weird name." Mary favors Blue both to honor Red and to express a unique individuality: "Because everyone is named Jill. And she's not like everyone." Ruhl stipulates an invisible Blue, a child as blank as the two fortunes that Mary unwraps in the Chinese restaurant, ones that invite strange and beautiful futures. Ruhl advances Blue's androgyny as a state of creative opportunity rather than confusion.

PASSION PLAY, A CYCLE IN THREE PARTS

Passion Play is Ruhl's most ambitious work to date. Each of its three parts depicts the staging of a historical Passion Play, and the totality spans from Elizabethan England to the present day and runs some three and a half hours. Ruhl began writing the first part, which served as her undergraduate thesis at Brown University under the auspices of Paula Vogel, twelve years before the premiere of the revised cycle at the Goodman Theatre in Chicago in fall 2007 under the direction of Mark Wing-Davey. Ruhl describes its genesis in her interview with Svich:

Passion Play came from a tiny idea. I thought: what if someone who played Pontius Pilate all his life wanted to play the role of Christ, played by his cousin? I had been traveling in England and brought with me a prized possession, a children's book called *Betsy and the Great World*. Perhaps this is not the place to publicize my fanatical love of the Betsy-Tacy series, but nevertheless, it was that book, with its travelogue of Betsy's pre-WWI trip to Oberammergau, Bavaria, that gave rise to the play. In Betsy's romp through Oberammergau, all the actors she meets are actually so holy as to embody the living picture of the New Testament.

I got to thinking: what if the woman playing the Virgin Mary were not quite as pure as her presentation might suggest? What if the actor playing Christ were a megalomaniac? As it turns out, Hitler came to the Oberammergau Passion in 1934 and was greeted with jubilation. . . . By the end of WWII, the entire village of Oberammergau had joined the Nazi party, with the exception of the actors who played Judas and Pilate. After having learned that information, I felt I couldn't end the play in the sixteenth century, which is how the first act ends. The Elizabethan's struggle with religious representation is only the beginning of a story that gets much darker in the twentieth century.

Following this scheme, in the first part of the cycle the character who plays Pilate envies his cousin, who plays Christ; in the second, Hitler visits Oberammergau; and in the third, the actor who plays Christ narcissistically advances his career. Ruhl began the second part while still an undergraduate at Brown University. The first part was awarded the Fourth Freedom Forum Playwriting Award through the Kennedy Center American College Theatre Festival and thus qualified for a reading at the Sundance Theater Laboratory in 2000.

The Sundance reading caught the attention of director Wing-Davey, who was there working on Naomi Iizuka's *36 Views*. He notes that he was "struck" by Ruhl's play, "by the language and its approach, by its particular voice." He subsequently staged the first two parts of *Passion Play* at the Actor's Centre, a small theater in London, on a budget of one hundred pounds. The one-week run was extended, and replacements found for those with prior commitments, when "the actors all fell in love with the play," as Wing-Davey states in the interview "Directing *Passion Play*." Artistic Director Molly Smith staged the entire cycle in 2005 at Arena Stage in Washington, D.C., which commissioned the third part. In an interview in *Onstage*, Ruhl regrets that she "didn't have time to quite finish the third act," which she would later revise for the Goodman production.

Each part depicts the staging of a Passion Play from a different historical period: Elizabethan England in 1575; Oberammergau, Germany, in 1934; and Spearfish, South Dakota, from 1969 to the present day. According to Ruhl, about one hundred villages would have been presenting the Passion in 1575; during that year, Queen Elizabeth banned all religious plays due to their Catholic associations. Hitler attended the Oberammergau Passion twice in 1934 and praised its anti-Semitism. The Bavarian production fulfills a pledge made to God in 1633 that, in exchange for protection from the plague, the townspeople would mount a Passion Play every ten years. The tradition continues to this day, as does that of the Spearfish, South Dakota, production. Known as the Black Hills Passion Play, it was established in 1939 by Josef Meier, a German immigrant who had led a touring version in the United States starting in 1932. As Tom Creamer notes in *Onstage*, Ruhl has chosen the settings with "great care" at periods of "great political charge" that were "each dominated by figures able to imprint their personalities on history." Ruhl stages Queen Elizabeth, Adolph Hitler, and Ronald Reagan and observes that, "each of those three figures addresses questions of how powerful people use theater to make things happen; how they use the same tricks that actors do to be liked and to control politics." She wishes to explore "the relationship of community to political icons."

Characters play the same biblical figure throughout the cycle and conform to or diverge from their role to varying degrees from part to part. As she began working on the play, Ruhl reports: "I started thinking, how would it shape or misshape a life to play a biblical role year after year?" In Part One, Mary 1 fails to safeguard her chastity and remain true to her virginal namesake. She lusts after the actor playing Jesus and wanders outside at night in search of male companionship. Impregnated by the actor playing Pilate, and in despair over her unworthiness in the eyes of God, she drowns herself. That actor, appropriately enough named Pontius, conforms to his part in that he hates his good-looking and virtuous cousin John, who plays Jesus.

The second part highlights the anti-Semitic nature of the Oberammergau Passion Play. The Village Idiot of the first part has become Violet, an orphaned Jewish girl. The soldier Eric, who plays Jesus, captures her for internment in a concentration camp. The actress playing the Virgin Mary, here named Elsa, submits to a German officer's advances. The Foot Soldier, playing Pontius, flirts with Eric; the German officer witnesses this and threatens them. Thus both Jewishness and homosexuality are identified as targets of Hitler's regime.

In the third part, the actors playing Pilate, called P, and Jesus, called J, are now brothers competing for the love of the former's wife. P returns from Vietnam a broken man. Meanwhile, his brother J has achieved celebrity as a soap opera star. While P is overseas, J sleeps with his wife, Mary 1, obscuring the paternity of her daughter, Violet. J pushes to professionalize and commercialize the Passion Play, to which ends the Young Director, a draft dodger with a fake English accent, is hired; he tangles with P, who rejoins the production after his tour of duty. This section spans from 1969 to the present day and includes a number of appearances by Ronald Reagan.

Ruhl establishes a rich set of images in the first part, upon which she draws in the second and third; much of this imagery is derived from biblical and Christian symbology, some of it associated with

Revelation and Apocalypse. These images include fish, water, the moon, a red sky, and birds and air. Ruhl added the third part of *Passion Play* in response to Arena Stage's request for a play about America. She found this "a daunting task" until she realized that "little is more American than the nexus of religious rhetoric, politics, and theatricality." In terms of her own religious beliefs, Ruhl has related to Lawrence Goodman that, although raised Catholic, she abandoned the faith as a teenager "after she'd decided it was unfair that priests, but not nuns, were the only ones allowed to communicate directly with God." A resistance to the patriarchal aspects of Christianity may be discerned in the attitudes of two female characters in *In the Next Room (or the vibrator play)*. As she grieves her deceased infant, the wet nurse, Elizabeth, imagines God's cabinet filled with "babies who get returned," who are inconsolable even within the arms of God the Father, crying for their earthly mothers. Unable to produce milk for her baby, Mrs. Givings ponders nursing and childbirth:

> Isn't it strange about Jesus? That is to say, about Jesus being a man? For it is women who are eaten — who turn their bodies into food — I gave up my blood — there was so much blood — and I gave up my body — but I couldn't feed her, could not turn my body into food, and she was so hungry. I suppose that makes me an inferior kind of woman and a very inferior kind of Jesus.

Or perhaps, by implication, the maleness of the Father and Son makes them inferior kinds of mothers, a role better left to the Virgin Mary.

In the interview with Reid, Ruhl ascribes her affinity for "weird transformations" to her Catholic heritage: "I come from a Catholic upbringing so I can talk about water turning into wine." Although she has not publicly articulated her current spiritual or religious beliefs, an agnostic humanism undergirds her plays. A high value is placed on human connection, as that between a father and daughter, a husband and wife, a sister and brother, or between lovers. Nevertheless, her characters exist within a greater spiritual realm. At the conclusion of *The Clean House*, a yew tree, representative of the tree of life that connects all levels of existence, rests on the stage as Matilde relates her vision of a heaven filled with laughter. Although he has rejected organized religion, P ascends to the sky in a sailing ship at the end of *Passion Play*. Ruhl's employment of magic realism in and of itself belies a faith in the existence of the numinous, in spite of her apparent rejection of organized religion.

IN THE NEXT ROOM (OR THE VIBRATOR PLAY)

In the Next Room (or the vibrator play) premiered at Berkeley Repertory Theatre in February 2009 and introduced Ruhl to Broadway in November of the same year. Both productions were directed by Les Waters. This work is situated in a spa town outside New York City during the Victorian era, at the dawn of the age of electricity. The set consists of two rooms in the house of Dr. Givings and his wife, Catherine: the living room and the room in which the doctor treats his patients. The boundary between the two is more permeable than the doctor would like. Scenes occur simultaneously in both rooms throughout. Fascinated with electricity, the doctor experiments with treating his patients with the newly invented vibrator, a device regarded at this time as having a purely clinical function. He applies it to his female patients to cure hysteria, a catchall diagnosis, by presumably decongesting the womb. Unhappy in her marriage and frustrated at being unable to produce milk for her baby, Catherine eavesdrops on her husband's treatments. Curious, she and a patient, Sabrina, break into his office to experiment with the new device. Catherine recognizes its sexual nature, but her husband is appalled when she brings this to his attention.

Dr. Givings applies the treatment to an artist who is suffering from what he diagnoses as a rare form of male hysteria. Catherine falls in love with the artist, who is white, and he in turn falls in love with Elizabeth, the black and married wet nurse, whom he paints as the Virgin Mother. Sabrina experiences feelings for, and shares a kiss with, Dr. Givings' assistant, Annie, a woman in her late thirties who has never married. However, these transgressive sexualities are quickly pushed behind the drapes of Victorian society; the artist flees to Paris to escape the racism he witnesses in America, and Sabrina and Annie agree that they must never see each other again. Catherine finally breaks through to her husband, and as the play concludes, they share a moment of intimacy in Catherine's snow-covered winter garden.

This work stages a sexual revolution of sorts within the marriage of the Givings, while also demonstrating the sexual intolerance prevalent in the late 1800s. Marriage both constrains and nurtures the female characters. Catherine is frustrated at the lack of opportunities for productive activity and the lack of intimacy in her marriage; she eventually overcomes at least the latter shortcoming. Although materially cared for, the sensitive Sabrina is trapped with her rather coarse, albeit solicitous, husband. The wet nurse, Elizabeth, is employed to nurture Catherine's baby while grieving the loss of her own. She is doubly constrained by both gender and race. Although her husband does not appear as a character, he is conveyed as being solicitous and tender. Nevertheless, her opportunities for employment are severely limited within a paternalistic and racist society.

Ruhl explores a number of themes, one of which is the interrelationship between sexuality and love. The legacy of slavery is expressed through the nurturing of Catherine's baby with the milk produced by Elizabeth for her deceased child; the white body is sustained by the output of the black one. Catherine links the Christian sacrament to breast-feeding, in which the baby consumes the body of the mother. Elizabeth has abandoned her faith at the death of her child. What sustains the characters are their connections to one another and the ensuing tenderness. Leo expresses this in terms of light:

> I love this time of the afternoon, when the world is becoming
> dark, and you can see outside your window — lights in the
> neighboring windows coming on. One yellow — one almost
> white — the squares of light, other people's lives — sheltered
> against the night, so hopeful. Ridiculous, isn't it, to have so
> much hope, to think a little square of light could blot out the
> darkness — and yet — another one comes on — and see . . .

Light assumes many meanings, as a symbol of progress associated with electricity, as a glaring side effect of intrusive technology, and as knowledge. The characters cannot resist clicking on and off the electric lamp, a novelty, in the living room, let alone the vibrator in the next room, toying as it were with the promise and threat of a technological future. Ruhl envisions this play as a companion piece to *Dead Man's Cell Phone*, as both are concerned with the benefits and dangers of technology. Ultimately, however, in both cases the gadgets are left behind during moments of deepest intimacy.

OTHER WORKS

Ruhl's other works include the short *Dog Play*, a study in grief that predates *Eurydice*; *Orlando*, a full-length adaptation of Virginia Woolf's novel of the same name; *Anna Around the Neck* and *The Lady with the Lapdog*, both one-act adaptations of two of Anton Chekhov's short stories and an adaptation of his play *The Three Sisters*; *Virtual Meditation #1*, a multimedia, interactive piece realized with the assistance of students from Carnegie Mellon University's Entertainment Technology Center; *Demeter in the City*, a Cornerstone Theater commission based on the lives of twenty-year-olds living in Los Angeles and structured around the Greek myth; and *Snowless*, a one-act that draws attention to global warming.

Dog Play

In 1998, Ruhl's *Dog Play* was given a reading at the Ten Minute Play Festival at Chicago Dramatists. Clearly derived from the exercise written for Vogel in 1994, the play explores the death of a father from the perspective of the family dog and lays the foundation for the later *Eurydice*. The lights come up on "a huge glowing puppet of a moon" to the sound of "a dog baying as though his heart is breaking." The title character, played by a male or female actor in a mask, washes the dishes and remembers the paramedics recently taking the father away. It turns out that the deceased father has been staying mostly in the moon. He converses solely with the dog, as no one else is able to see him, including the daughter, who desperately wishes to do so. The mood is dreamlike and, at times, nightmarish. A doctor looks into the daughter's mouth while she tells a sad story to see if she is crying inside. As the family fishes together, "someone catches something huge, and everyone screams in terror, turning in slow motion to the audience"; it turns out to be the family dog, hooked in the mouth. As a group of mourners follows the moon, baying at it, subtitles relate a mundane conversation about funeral arrangements.

Whereas in *Eurydice*, Ruhl depicts various stages of the bereavement process, in *Dog Play* she focuses on the sense of shock and unreality that occurs immediately after the loss. The earlier play is rawer and more condensed. Ruhl demonstrates an early interest in theatricality and a disregard for realist convention. Dog and human ways of mourning are juxtaposed throughout, with the huge, puppet moon linking the two modes of perception. Dogs bay at the moon, where the deceased father is now living, to convey bereavement on the animal level. Yet the dog also engages in civilized conversations with the father as they listen together to a jazz recording, complaining about the rude manners of other dogs:

I don't like to play with other dogs anymore. They just can't
seem to understand. I have my memories — they don't. They
exist in the eternal present and don't realize that the biting
and sniffing of genitalia is vulgar.

The dog assumes a humanness in its possession of memory, and the
theme of the centrality of memory to human life will be expanded on
in *Eurydice*. In *Dog Play*, Ruhl tries out themes that will be developed
at length in *Eurydice*; nevertheless, it does not read as an immature,
undeveloped work but stands strongly on its own merits.

Orlando

Joyce Piven commissioned Ruhl's adaptation of the Virginia Woolf
novel and directed it at the Piven Theater Workshop in 1998 and subsequently at the Actor's Gang in Los Angeles in 2003. The novel, and
play, follows Orlando through three centuries, including his transformation from male to female. Ruhl includes the protagonist's major
love relationships, his brief encounter with Shakespeare, and his/her
musings on gender and ongoing effort to write a poem about an oak
tree. Orlando and Sasha are played by women, with a chorus assuming
all other roles. The play is composed as a mixture of narrative and
dialogue, with Orlando and the chorus sharing the role of narrator.
Ruhl preserves the verbal playfulness of the novel as is consistent with
her own style, one perhaps originally inspired, at least in part, by
Woolf. In the play and in the novel, for example, when Orlando first
sees, and instantly falls in love with, the Russian Princess Sasha, he calls
out, in his astonishment, a seemingly unrelated list of objects: "melon,
pineapple, olive tree, emerald, fox in the snow." Ruhl also shares
Woolf's whimsicality, in evidence in the novelist's description of the
great freeze of London as delivered by Ruhl's chorus:

Birds froze in mid-air
and fell like stones to the ground.

It was no uncommon sight to come upon
a whole herd of swine frozen immovable upon the road. . . .
The ice went so deep and so clear that there could
be seen, congealed at a depth of a few thousand feet, here a
porpoise, there a flounder!!!

This playful whimsicality runs throughout both play and novel.

Chekhov Adaptations

When pressed by interviewer Peter Gianopulos to sum up the thematic essence of her work, Ruhl responded with "love and death." In
her two adaptations of Chekhov short stories, the focus is on love or
the lack of it. Joyce Piven commissioned and directed these adaptations as well and presented them as part of the program *Chekhov:
The Stories* in March 2000. In these adaptations, as in *Orlando*, characters switch between representational and presentational modes,
engaging in dialogue as well as narration. One of the adaptations
includes a proper chorus, out of which various characters emerge, and
the other contains two generic characters that fulfill a choric function.

Chekhov's short story "The Lady with the Lap Dog" chronicles
an affair between Gurov, a middle-aged man, and Anna, a young
woman, both of whom are married. In each other, they find an intimacy
and excitement that is lacking in their otherwise unhappy and mundane lives. Ruhl faithfully reproduces the ambiguous conclusion,
having her characters speak as Chekhov's narrator:

> GUROV: And it seemed as though in a little while the solution
> would be found, and that a new and glorious life would
> begin for them.
> ANNA: It was clear to both of them that the end was still far
> off, and the hardest and most complicated part was only
> just beginning.

The second short-story adaptation, *Anna Around the Neck*, also features a spring-autumn relationship, an unhappy marriage between eighteen-year-old Anna and fifty-two-year-old Modest Alexeich. Anna has married for money, her mother having passed away and her alcoholic father barely able to provide for Anna and her two brothers. She finds herself intimidated by her husband, a dull and unappealing but well-off government official, who keeps her in a state of virtual poverty. She comes into her own, however, when she is introduced to high society, which she dazzles with her beauty and grace. After this coming-out, she is able to demand of her husband that all of her financial needs be met, as he recognizes both her newly found influence and power as well as the benefits of having such a charming and popular wife.

Anna's transformation changes her relationship with her family as well. Although in the early stages of her marriage she dines with her father and brothers daily at their home, she later ceases to visit them. At the conclusion of both play and story, as she passes her father and brothers on the street in a carriage, the embarrassed sons prevent the father from calling out to her.

Ruhl also adapted Chekhov's full-length play *The Three Sisters*. The adaptation was commissioned by and premiered at the Cincinnati Playhouse in October 2009 under the direction of John Doyle.

Virtual Meditation #1

As with the Chekhov adaptations, love is the theme of *Virtual Meditation #1*. The Actors Theatre of Louisville commissioned and produced it as part of the Humana Festival of New American Plays in March 2002. Brenda Harger directed, and students at Carnegie Mellon University's Entertainment Technology Center programmed the technical elements. The play was remounted at Carnegie Mellon University in April and May of the same year. To begin, two audience members, who may or may not know one another, are randomly selected. They are digitally photographed, recorded stating their names, seated on a bench and attached to a monitor that records the beating of their hearts, and asked to hold hands.

The play consists of three scenes. Throughout, digital images of the participants' faces are projected onto the faces of mannequins. These facial images have been programmed to represent various emotions that change according to stage directions in the script. Actors have pre-recorded a dialogue into which are inserted the participants' names. The play charts the course of a relationship: The characters introduce themselves to one another in the first scene, and by the third they are discussing marriage. The three settings are a park, a museum, and a moon-lit lake. A screen behind the mannequins projects various images that are influenced by the volunteers' heartbeats and the pressure of their hand holding. The sensory input influences the rate of rain, a quantity of tulips, the saturation and proximity of bands of colors in a Rothko painting, the number of ripples in a lake, and the brightness of the moon.

The dialogue is simple throughout, and the piece relies on sophisticated computer programming. As of the date of this writing, a brief documentary about the performance is available at the Carnegie Mellon University site for the project. It chronicles the arrival of the audience, the selecting of volunteers, and the hooking up of the monitors, and shows clips from the performance. The last few minutes of the documentary focus on the interactions between various sets of volunteers (the performance was run numerous times), a significant facet of the performance, as two people, possibly strangers, were brought together and their reactions observed by the audience.

Demeter in the City

Cornerstone Theater commissioned Ruhl to write a play about twenty-year-olds in Los Angeles; it was presented at REDCAT in June 2006 under the direction of Shishir Kurup. Ruhl considers the script to still be a work-in-progress. The playwright interviewed young people across the city, including "young mothers in a program called Shields

Healthy Start in Compton. . . . ROTC students, young Republicans at UCLA, undergraduates at USC, activists in Movimiento Estudiantil Chicano de Aztlá at Cal State Northridge, social workers, and young people recently emancipated from foster care." She found that many subjects were concerned about the separation between parents and children and the struggle to define oneself after leaving home. Ruhl found that the myth of Demeter and Persephone resonated with the young mothers at Shields Healthy Start, many of whom had lost their children to foster care due to drug addiction. In the Greek myth, mother and daughter are separated when Hades steals Persephone away to the underworld; in her despair, Demeter, the goddess of agriculture, neglects the earth's crops. To avert famine, Zeus intervenes, and a compromise is reached wherein Persephone spends half her time on earth and half in the underworld, with these times corresponding to summer and winter.

Ruhl structures her plot on this myth. Demeter is a young mother whose child is taken into foster care after a social worker finds used heroin needles in her apartment. The judge fulfills the role of Zeus, and a Young Republican that of Hades, who seduces a now twenty-year-old Persephone at the beginning of the second act and whisks her away to the underworld. After twenty years, Demeter has recovered from her addiction and tracks down Zeus, now retired, in a gated community in Palm Springs. The central characters, including Hermes, who was the bailiff and is now Zeus' driver, come to realize that they are indeed Greek gods. Zeus works out the compromise, and Persephone is reunited with her mother. The play draws attention to the plight of drug-addicted mothers who have lost their children, indicting the foster care system without exonerating the mothers. It focuses on the human toll caused by the separation of parent and child. The work is Brechtian in nature, highlighting political and social issues and commenting on the action through song. The use of a Greek chorus, consisting of "at least three mothers, all different ethnicities," contributes to the alienation effect. Whereas Ruhl adapts Greek myth in *Eurydice* to stage personal grief, in *Demeter in the City*, myth is used for a more overtly political purpose.

Snowless

Snowless, a one-act play, first appeared at the Chicago Humanities Festival in November 2007, then at the New York University Humanities Festival in April 2008; in both instances, playbills indicate the plays are concerned with global warming. The first of two scenes, set "sometime in the future," consists of a conversation between two groups of three characters each, one composed of "older, one might even say, ancient" characters, the other of children. As the title suggests, snow no longer occurs. The older characters attempt to describe snow and its effects to the children. As the scene progresses, water rises from the characters' toes to their chins.

At the beginning of the second scene, an older couple sits over breakfast as the Woman reads aloud a *New York Times* article concerning climate change. The article includes the statistic that the honeybee population has declined by 70 percent. Absorbed in his own reading, the Man fails to respond to his wife's growing sense of alarm until a bee buzzes through the window and stings him on the arm. At this point the Woman calls on their Belgian beekeeping neighbor, Maurice, for advice about bees. Maurice quotes at length from Maurice Maeterlinck's *The Life of the Bee*. In a sudden plot twist characteristic of Ruhl, Maurice and the Woman lie down together in the garden and, before long, start kissing. Snow begins to fall. Three grandchildren appear in the garden, and the voices of the three ancients from the first scene once again relate memories of snow. In unison, and in what appears to be an homage to the children's book *Goodnight Moon*, a work that Ruhl reports having read to her daughter, all the characters wish good night to a long list of things, including snow, bees, elephants, and trees. The sound of the bees grows louder, then falls silent, as a blackout ends the play.

The play is unusual for its inclusion of long passages from a work of nonfiction. These passages from Maeterlinck serve to educate the audience about bees and provide instructions for how to best address the threat of global warming:

> Just as it is written on the tongue, the stomach, and the mouth of the bee that it must make honey, so it is written in our eyes, our ears, our nerves, our marrow, that we must make this — how do you call it — cerebral substance — nor must we know the purpose the substance shall serve.

In a touch of magic realism, the kissing of the Woman and Maurice produces snow in May, in reference to which the Woman claims that she is making honey for her grandchildren and their descendants. The play optimistically suggests that human ingenuity will solve the problems posed by global warming.

HER PLACE IN AMERICAN DRAMA

It is no doubt too early to position Ruhl definitively within American drama. Nevertheless, it is possible to discern affinities with other American playwrights and further illuminate her body of work by comparison. Ruhl's lineage may be traced back through Tony Kushner to John Guare and Thornton Wilder. Each of these playwrights resists the tendency toward realism that has dominated the twentieth and, so far, twenty-first century. The theories of Bertolt Brecht serve as a useful touchstone when discussing these dramatists. Brecht deliberately reminds the spectator that he or she is witnessing a play, in contrast to realists, who strive to immerse the viewer in an illusion of everyday life. Techniques used in the service of *verfremdungseffekt*, or the alienation effect, include direct address and "songs, scenic titles, projected slides and an almost completely bare stage," as expressed by Charles H. Helmetag in his article in *Modern Language Studies*.

Wilder would almost certainly have been familiar with Brecht's practice and writings and goes to great lengths in his own works to destroy theatrical illusion. Lacking Brecht's political agenda, Wilder rather employs these techniques to illuminate archetype. Kushner, the most political of the American playwrights under discussion, acknowledges a great debt to Brecht, as the title of his interview with Carl Weber, "I Always Go Back to Brecht," indicates. He has called for an American form of Brechtianism, and if anyone has achieved this, it has been Kushner in his *Angels in America*, with its focus on the AIDS crisis and the American religion of Mormonism.

Guare's application of Brechtian techniques, such as song and direct address, shows more of an affinity with Wilder than with Kushner, as his concerns lie with the archetype of the little man pursuing the American dream rather than with any overtly political agenda. He paints on a smaller canvas than does Wilder, detailing the angst and neuroses of his characters rather than sketching the world at large. Ruhl has used all the Brechtian techniques listed above in various combinations. Like Wilder, she captures the big picture, often inclusive of an afterlife, while at the same time conveying an intimate sense of character, as does Guare. Even a Ruhl play that incorporates political figures, such as *Passion Play*, tends more toward the personal and metaphysical than political. Unfettered by the conventions of realism, these playwrights are free to venture into metaphysical geographies, something that Ruhl, Wilder, and Kushner do frequently and with enthusiasm. Ruhl, Wilder, and Guare craft poetic dialogue, wringing new connotations out of words and arranging them in startling juxtapositions. Although Kushner certainly writes commanding dialogue, it is typically in a conversational rather than poetic mode.

WILDER'S TOWN

Fittingly, John Guare provides the introduction to the first volume of Thornton Wilder's collected short plays. In it, Guare discusses Wilder's attempt to rebirth language, to rescue words from the weight of a literary tradition that burdens them with an accretion of meaning. Wilder drew inspiration in this endeavor from Gertrude Stein, whom he met when she lectured at the University of Chicago in 1935, at his invitation, and with whom he formed a close friendship. As cited by Guare, Stein exhorted the artist to reinstill the "excitingness of pure being" into what had become "stale literary words," advice that Wilder took to heart. According to Guare, she "validated his gift of capturing the poetry of common speech," and Guare gives as an example this line from the Wilder short play *The Happy Journey to Trenton and Camden*: "Goodness, smell that air, will you! It's got the whole ocean in it. — Elmer, drive careful over that bridge." Although Guare refrains from analyzing this line, it clearly operates as poetry in its employment of both image and juxtaposition: the air contains the "whole ocean," and the character abruptly switches from marveling at this to monitoring her husband's driving. This sudden zoom in from the vast to the mundane demonstrates Wilder's overarching goal to situate the banalities of everyday American life within the greater patterns of the cosmos.

Ruhl likewise juxtaposes words to keep them fresh, as when Matilde characterizes the perfect joke as existing "somewhere between an angel and a fart." In another example, the Other Woman exhorts Jean to become comfortable with putting on makeup in public:

JEAN: I've always been embarrassed to put lipstick on in public.
OTHER WOMAN: That's crap. Here — You have beautiful lips.

The word *crap* clashes humorously with *beautiful lips*. Ruhl's style is defined, as much as anything, by unusual, startling, and whimsical imagery such as this, expressed poetically and with humor. Instances abound in *Eurydice*: The Nasty Interesting Man scoffs at Orpheus' "long fingers that would tremble to pet a bull or pluck a bee from a hive," fingers that compare unfavorably to his own "big stupid hands like potatoes"; the Loud Stone conveys the hushed language of the dead: "Like if the pores in your face / opened up and talked"; and Orpheus dreams of Eurydice's hair as streaming faucets.

Wilder once again drew support from Gertrude Stein in his belief that America occupies a special place in history through an identification with world destiny. The American thus stands for humanity as a whole as Wilder attempts to place the archetypal American in relation to the cosmos. In *Our Town*, which premiered in 1938, the residents of Grover's Corners, New Hampshire, pass through life's phases at the turn of the twentieth century. As Wilder states in the preface to *Three Plays*, his goal in this work is "to find a value above all price for the smallest events in our daily life." He reaches for the universal through the details of small-town America, and to this end his characters are types from that domain: the town doctor, the editor of the local paper, the milkman, the town drunkard. The foibles and humanity of these characters imbues Wilder's grand, universalist vision with a sense of irony.

The theme of an American identification with world destiny comes through clearly in Wilder's *The Skin of Our Teeth*, which premiered in October 1942. The Antrobuses function as the primal and archetypal family. Mr. Antrobus is credited with major human accomplishments such as the invention of the wheel and discovery of the times tables. The son, Henry, has killed his brother with a rock and is associated with Cain specifically and human evil in general. Wilder purposefully jumbles human and natural history, challenging the family with an ice age, the biblical flood, and a modern war. They survive through perseverance and ingenuity, which are arguably American attributes, but more generally human ones as well. Again, Wilder conveys a sense of irony through his portrayal of his figures as human and oftentimes comic. As just one example, he endows Mr. Antrobus with the "face of a Keystone Comedy Cop." The interconnectedness of American and world destiny has been undeniable at least since the time of the premiere, occurring as it did less than a year after the United States' entry into World War II.

Ruhl is also greatly concerned with archetype, although in a different way. Wilder can perhaps best be categorized as a Christian humanist and accordingly situates his American characters in a biblical cosmos. Although raised Catholic, Ruhl does not claim any particular religious affinity, as discussed above, and the worlds of her plays do not reflect the philosophy of any specific faith or denomination. Whereas Wilder sets out to demonstrate a relationship between character/archetype and cosmos, Ruhl shapes the myth to suit her purpose. In *Eurydice*, she fashions a personalized portrait of bereavement. In *Demeter in the City*, she cobbles together stories of twenty-year-old Los Angelenos, focusing on drug-addicted mothers who have had their children taken away from them. With *Passion Play*, Ruhl draws on the story of Christ while producing a work that is neither pro- nor anti-Christian. Rather, the consequences of either emulating or resisting the archetype are examined. Whereas the Antrobuses match the pattern of the original biblical family, the "actors" in *Passion Play* respond to, rather than exemplify, the archetype. For example, in the third part of *Passion Play*, the character P attempts to reconcile his portrayal of Pontius with the role that he played as a soldier in Vietnam as he talks with his wife:

> P: I was powering a ship that had a gunner on the back. And one time, we heard this huge explosion, and people were wounded, and we went ashore to help out. I was holding a little girl — about Violet's age. And her head was in my hands, and it was wet, and I realized her whole skull was — and her brains, in my hands — on my clothes — and for a long time we thought the enemy shot into that truck, because we thought who would kill women and children like that — it must have been them — but later I realized

no — there were no other explosions — we were shooting
into the woodline. It was us.

MARY 1: It's not your fault.

P: There were no showers, you know — we were in country on
February 28th — I didn't shower until May 10th. I washed
my hands without water.

(He rubs his hands together.)

P: Pontius Pilate — with no water.

MARY 1: Honey.

P: And I would think of old Pilate, lying there in the dark. How
Pilate was good — he had to kill someone innocent, it was
all part of the big plan. He saved us all, didn't he, by being
willing to be bad. But — a little girl's brains — there is no
plan — for that.

MARY 1: You're a good man.

P: Would you lie to me because you felt sorry for me?

MARY 1: No.

P: I don't want to be in the play anymore.

Here, Ruhl employs a biblical archetype to serve her goals within a
particular play, as opposed to Wilder, who does so to situate his
characters within a Christian universe.

For both Ruhl and Wilder, stage reality encompasses both the
living and the dead. In *Our Town*, Wilder has borrowed his vision of
the afterlife from Dante's *Purgatory*. The cemetery, home to the dead
and Emily's resting place, functions architecturally as part of the
greater structure of town and cosmos. In Ruhl, the afterlife catalyzes
personal transition. Like Emily, Eurydice comes to prefer the land of
the dead to that of the living; however, she does so because of the
presence there of her father. She vocalizes her preference as the
Chorus of Stones urges her to rejoin her husband:

LITTLE STONE: You can't go back now, Eurydice.

LOUD STONE: Face forward!

BIG STONE: Keep walking.

EURYDICE: I'm afraid!

LOUD STONE: Your husband is waiting for you, Eurydice.

EURYDICE: I don't recognize him! That's a stranger!

LITTLE STONE: Go on. It's him.

EURYDICE: I want to go home! I want my father!

LOUD STONE: You're all grown up now. You have a husband.

Shortly thereafter, Eurydice calls out Orpheus' name as he attempts to lead her out of the underworld, thereby sabotaging his attempt in order to remain with her father. In *The Clean House* and *Dead Man's Cell Phone*, the dead push the living back toward life. Matilde's parents cease to haunt her once she accepts their loss, and Jean's quick visit to hell convinces her that she is in love with the wrong man.

SIMILARITIES TO GUARE AND KUSHNER

Like Ruhl and Wilder, John Guare is a nonrealist with a poetic style. Isolation is a frequent theme of his. Many of his characters pursue celebrity and/or the American dream and in doing so are drawn away from living in the present moment; their obsessions prevent them from establishing meaningful relationships and thus result in alienation. In the introduction to his interview with Guare, David Savran observes that, in Guare's plays: "Events never turn out as planned, his characters never get what they want and yet, almost inevitably, they turn their losses into unexpected gain." The same may be said of Ruhl's works, which almost always end hopefully.

Savran compares Guare's detailed plot construction to that of Chekhov:

Guare stands out among his contemporaries for his intricately plot-driven playwriting, filled with both the major reversals and the little ironic surprises — so common in Chekhov — that force characters incessantly to reevaluate their situations.

Ruhl's works follow the same pattern; her protagonists constantly adapt to often ironic shifts in the environment. Indeed, her affinity for Chekhov is evident in her adaptations of his short stories and *The Three Sisters*.

Like Guare, Ruhl specializes in quirky scenarios: the chorus of stones in the underworld, whose lord is a petulant child who grows to be ten feet tall; the housekeeper who hates to clean; the shy woman who commandeers a dead man's cell phone; and the spurned lover who transforms into an almond, to name a few. And yet there is a qualitative difference between the quirkiness, and indeed the overall tone, of the two playwrights. In Guare, the characters tend to talk past each other, wrapped up as they are in their own fantasies. In Ruhl, the characters ultimately succeed in connecting with one another. Eurydice defies the Stones and reestablishes her relationship with her father, a community of women gathers to nurse Ana, Jean ultimately unites with the gentler brother, and the characters in *Melancholy Play* celebrate becoming almonds together. Guare's world is colder and has sharper edges. Whereas Ruhl's characters love and sometimes lose, Guare's oftentimes never truly love.

In a preview by Graydon Royce, Ruhl claims to be more of a Jungian than a Freudian:

> I don't love everything Jung said but in terms of universality as opposed to individual neurosis, in explaining things, I'm more interested in that onstage. Our theater has been in the post-Freudian world for so long, with our theater being about explaining why individuals are wounded and bizarre

because of secrets they carry with them. I'm more interested in the Jungian sense of commonality.

The use of joke as incantation in *The Clean House*, with its invocation of shamanism, demonstrates this Jungian bias. In *Dead Man's Cell Phone*, Jean's voyage to the underworld to encounter Gordon may be read as the kind protagonist's encounter with her own animus or male aspect, or dark side, from which she emerges whole and free to couple with Dwight. The reliance on archetype, so common in Ruhl's plays, is another indication of a Jungian disposition. In most of his works, Guare features the Freudian, wounded individual that Ruhl finds unappealing. Although Guare and Ruhl's styles are similar in a number of ways, the difference in underlying psychological model is a significant distinguishing factor.

As do Guare, Ruhl, and Wilder, Kushner creates nonrealistic theater and incorporates realms beyond the ordinary. His work is the most overtly political of the four playwrights under discussion. His employment of the celestial realm in *Angels in America* serves as a reminder of the overriding importance of human agency, functioning in a Brechtian sense as a prod for audience action in the political realm. Ruhl's deployment of the supernatural differs from that of both Kushner and Wilder. In her works, the afterworld is a place of reconnection and mourning, as in *Eurydice*, or a place in which illusions are set aside, as in *Dead Man's Cell Phone*. In *The Clean House*, Matilde envisions it as a place of uncomprehending mirth: "I think maybe heaven is a sea of untranslatable jokes. Only everyone is laughing." The afterlife in Ruhl functions predominantly on a personal level, rather than an overarching theological one as in Wilder, or in a political capacity as with Kushner.

AMERICAN DREAMS

What marks each of these playwrights as distinctly American, and how are they alike and different in this regard? Wilder grants the American a privileged position in the course of history and situates him in the cosmos as a representative of the human race, although he does so with a sense of irony. Guare locates his characters in a celebrity-obsessed culture and chronicles their disappointment and tenacity as they struggle to achieve the American dream. Kushner protests American politics, finding the Reagan Administration particularly abhorrent, as a reading of *Angels in America* confirms.

Ruhl usually sets her plays in America and deals with American concerns. Even in *Eurydice*, the father is a Midwesterner who equates the Mississippi with the River Lethe:

> FATHER: You'll see the lights on the Mississippi River.
> Take off your shoes.
> Walk down the hill.
> You'll pass a tree good for climbing on the right.
> Cross the road.
> Watch for traffic.
> Cross the train tracks.
> Catfish are sleeping in the mud, on your left.
> Roll up your jeans.
> Count to ten.
> Put your feet in the river
> and swim.
>
> *(He dips himself in the river. A small metallic sound of forget-fulness — ping. The sound of water. He lies down on the ground, curled up, asleep.)*

Yet she does not grant Americans as privileged a position in the cosmos as Wilder does. She contrasts American culture with that of Europe in *Melancholy Play*, and although Lorenzo, the European psychologist, is a rather ludicrous character, Ruhl also indicates that the cellist who underscores the action with haunting melodies should be "from a country other than the United States." She counterpoints the vapid absurdity of one non-American with the poignant musicality of another. The work promotes European melancholy over American depression as a mood to be savored rather than medicated away. Overall, she contrasts cultures in order to gently point out the virtues and foibles of each. Her work is less politicized than Kushner's. This may be demonstrated by comparing the play by each that focuses on domestic servitude, Kushner's musical *Caroline, or Change* against Ruhl's *The Clean House*. In Kushner, Caroline is a victim of a racist system; however, she herself lacks the will to fight. It is up to the next generation, in the person of her daughter, to engage in the Civil Rights movement. In Ruhl, the immigrant housekeeper integrates into a community of women across nationalistic and cultural boundaries. The characters change, but political change is not on the agenda.

Although Ruhl's characters do not pursue the American dream with the same ferocity as Guare's, nevertheless some do aspire to it and find it lacking. The seemingly perfect marriage of two successful doctors residing in a "metaphysical Connecticut" falls apart in *The Clean House*; a veteran returns home a broken man after serving his country in Vietnam in *Passion Play*; and in *Demeter in the City*, some of the less fortunate inhabitants of Los Angeles struggle to improve their lives. The American dream is not alive and well in these works, and the characters do not pursue that broken dream with the maniacal obsessiveness found in Guare. In *Bosoms and Neglect*, Deirdre quotes E. M. Forster's directive to "Connect. Only connect." In this regard, Guare's characters usually fail; Ruhl's, on the other hand, typically succeed.

THE FUTURE RUHL

Ruhl is only in her mid-thirties at the time of this writing, and perhaps her best work still lies ahead of her. She has apparently moved beyond writing plays of mourning, although one expects that the themes of love and death will continue to dominate her work. Her current works contain a larger measure of lightness than darkness. In his profile of

Ruhl in *The New Yorker*, John Lahr reports commenting to Mark Wing-Davey on the "oddness" of the "ironic detachment" and "unabashed optimism" of *Dead Man's Cell Phone*. The director replied, "Why shouldn't it be? [sic] . . . Right now Sarah's life is great — a young child, newly married, the darling of the American theatre scene, her plays are done." No matter what the tone, it may be expected that Ruhl will continue to draw on a wide range of subject matter and to create whimsical, intriguing works in her own unique voice.

Charles Isherwood of *The New York Times* has been a significant champion of Ruhl's work, particularly in his reviews of *Eurydice* and *The Clean House*. The awards that she has received attest to her importance within the world of American theater. These include a $500,000 MacArthur Foundation Fellowship in 2006 and the Helen Merrill and Whiting Writers' awards. *The Clean House* was awarded the $10,000 Susan Smith Blackburn Prize in 2003–04 (awarded for the best play in the English language by a woman), was a Pulitzer Prize finalist in 2005, and a 2005 PEN Award recipient. *Passion Play* received the Kennedy Center Fourth Forum Freedom Award. Annually in *American Theatre* (and on their Web site), Theatre Communications Group posts a list of the top ten most-produced works in U.S. regional theaters for the coming season; Ruhl's plays have made the list for three years running, through the 2009–10 season. Her work has been produced at numerous theaters, including the Goodman Theatre, Lincoln Center Theater, Second Stage, Yale Repertory Theatre, Woolly Mammoth Theatre Company, Berkeley Repertory Theater, the Piven Theatre Workshop, and the Steppenwolf Theater. Her plays have been translated into German, Polish, Korean, Russian, and Spanish and have been produced outside the United States in Britain, Canada, Germany, Latvia, Poland, New Zealand, and Australia. The theater world can anticipate that this young playwright will continue to write commercially successful and artistically fulfilling works for many years to come.

DRAMATIC MOMENTS

from the Major Plays

These short excerpts are from the playwright's major plays. They give a taste of the work of the playwright. Each has a short introduction in brackets that helps the reader understand the context of the excerpt. The excerpts, which are in chronological order, illustrate the main themes mentioned in the In an Hour essay.

from **Melancholy Play: a contemporary farce** (2002)
from Part Two, Scene 5

CHARACTERS

Lorenzo
Frank
Julian
Joan

[Each of the characters, in turn, falls in love with Tilly for her beautiful melancholy. When she becomes suddenly happy, they find her less appealing. In Part Two, Scene 5, her lover, Frank (a tailor), seeks psychiatric help from Lorenzo, who unbeknownst to Frank has treated, and is himself in love with, Tilly. Joan appears late in the scene seeking help for her lover, Frances, who is also in despair over Tilly's happiness. Julian is a character who plays cello accompaniment throughout the play. He does not speak until the final scene.]

LORENZO: Go on.
FRANK: I was hemming her pants, and I fell in love.
LORENZO: I know what love is!
FRANK: Excuse me?
LORENZO: Go on, go on.

(Lorenzo is distracted. He eats marzipan.)

FRANK: She was so beautiful — when she was sad — I couldn't help
    myself — I wanted to bathe in her sadness like a bath —
LORENZO: Of course you did.
FRANK: She would cry sometimes in her sleep.
        I put her tears in a little vial. I collected them.

LORENZO: Ah, like the Romans.

FRANK: What?

LORENZO: The Romans. Collected tears in little vials. Buried them with the dead.

FRANK: This vial is all I have left of her. Is that weird?

(Frank produces a vial of tears.)

LORENZO: Yes, it is weird. Would you like some candy? Marzipan. It's good.

FRANK: No, thank you. But you said the Romans did it.

LORENZO: Forget the Romans. Go on.

(Lorenzo eats marzipan.)

FRANK: I never loved someone so much. Now — she's gone — and I wish I were dead.

(Lorenzo laughs.)

FRANK: Why are you laughing?

LORENZO: Perhaps I'm laughing because, I, too, have felt the way that you feel, Frank.

FRANK: Oh.

LORENZO: You seem — depressed.

FRANK: Maybe a little.

LORENZO: It is my medical opinion that you should go on medication. It's a very good medication. It will make you feel — very nice.

FRANK: I am sad because I fell out of love. I am not sad like: "I want to take medication."

LORENZO: Frank. Maybe you should have a little stay at the hospital.

FRANK: I don't want to stay at a hospital! I think I will move to another country. In French movies, people *die* of love. They *die* of it.

LORENZO: Frank. Frank. Poor Frank. Why don't you continue with your story.

FRANK: Well — one day — all at once — with no explanation — she was — happy. Cheerful, even. It was like a violent accident. A car wreck. We suddenly had nothing in common. I felt — so far away from her. Her face got red when she was happy, like a sweaty cow. And her voice got louder. And her eyes got glazed over, like a sweaty cow.

LORENZO: Yes! And how did that make you feel?

FRANK: Well, Tilly came home from her birthday party —

LORENZO: Tilly?

FRANK: That's the woman's name. Tilly.

LORENZO: I was at Tilly's birthday party! Not you!

FRANK: You know Tilly?

LORENZO: Do I know Tilly? DO I KNOW TILLY!

FRANK: This is outrageous. *I* am paying *YOU*!

LORENZO: Give me that vial of tears.

FRANK: No!

LORENZO: Give it here!

FRANK: No! It's mine! It's mine! I collected them!

LORENZO: Her tears belong to me!

(Stirring fight music, from Julian. Frank and Lorenzo wrestle over the vial of tears. This wrestling goes on for a good minute, with much swearing, name-calling, and knocking over of furniture. Joan appears at the door. She knocks.)

JOAN: *(From outside)* Is anything wrong? *(She hears scuffling.)*

FRANK: Bastard!

LORENZO: Imbecile! Give it!

(Joan enters.)

JOAN: What's going on?

(Lorenzo wrestles Frank to the ground and sits astride him.)

LORENZO: Give me the vial or I will drool onto your face!

FRANK: I won't give it!

JOAN: *(Over the shouting)* Lorenzo? Are you a doctor? Who is the doctor and who is the patient?

LORENZO: I am now going to let saliva drop down from my mouth — if you give me the vial, I will suck the drool back up — now — now!

FRANK: I won't! I won't!

JOAN: Should I call security?

LORENZO: Leave me alone with my patient, please. Give me the vial, Frank. Give it up.

FRANK: Her tears are mine!

LORENZO: I'm going to drool!

FRANK: *(To Joan.)* I don't know who you are — but please — help me — take his vial — and run! Run! It belongs to a woman named Tilly —

(Frank reaches out toward Joan. Lorenzo pulls on Frank's legs. Joan takes the vial. She looks at the audience. A tableau. Strange music from Julian on his cello.)

****

from **Late: a cowboy song** (2003)
from Part Two, Scene 7

CHARACTERS

Crick

Mary

[Mary and Crick have been experiencing marital problems. In Part Two, Scene 7, Mary catches a ride home on a horse with Red, the female cowboy to whom she is becoming increasingly attached.]

Crick waits for Mary to come home. He looks at his watch. He looks at the magazines on the coffee table. He sees Mary's journal. He looks at the cover. He puts it down. He picks it up. He reads it. He is disturbed. He hears the sound of horse's hooves coming from outside. He looks out the window. He sees Mary riding up to the front door on a horse. Mary enters.

MARY: Hi.

CRICK: What the —

MARY: I got a ride.

CRICK: Yeah! I saw!

MARY: I got a ride home.

CRICK: Mary! Riding a horse to our *front* steps — as though that were a perfectly *natural* thing to do — JESUS GOD IN HEAVEN!

MARY: You'll wake the baby.

CRICK: So let's all wake up — you, me, the baby! Because, Mary, the unexamined life is not worth living. I've had it with your antics.

MARY: I haven't done anything wrong.

CRICK: You're late!

(He throws a pot against the wall.)

MARY: I know. I'm sorry.

CRICK: I've been waiting for you since the second grade.

MARY: You have me.

CRICK: A woman who *respects* her husband does not ride a *horse* up to his front door with another *man* —

MARY: Woman —

CRICK: For all the neighbors to see!

Who was that?

MARY: Red.

CRICK: It looked like a man.

MARY: I told you. She's a cowboy.

CRICK: I read your journal.

MARY: You what?

CRICK: I read your journal.

MARY: How could you?

CRICK: I was home all day, waiting for you. I wondered what you were thinking about. I thought maybe there was something nice in it — about us.

MARY: Did you read the whole thing?

CRICK: No.

MARY: What parts?

CRICK: You were riding a horse.

MARY: When?

CRICK: On Veteran's Day. You said you were home all day. Why did you lie to me?

MARY: I don't know. I was afraid.

CRICK: Why would you be afraid of me? Have I ever hurt you?

MARY: No.

CRICK: So then why?

MARY: I don't know.

CRICK: All I ever asked of you was a little honesty!

(He throws a loaf of bread against the wall. She starts crying.)

CRICK: Stop crying!

MARY: Why?

CRICK: I can't be mad at you if you're crying!

MARY: I'm sorry.

I'm going to my mother's.

CRICK: Don't go.

MARY: YOU READ MY JOURNAL!

CRICK: I'm sorry. That was bad of me.

MARY: You can't ever do that again.

CRICK: I won't. I promise. Mary — no one will ever love you as much as I love you.

(Kissing her.)

CRICK: I love you I love you I love you I love you I love you I love you.

MARY: I love you, too.

CRICK: You still leaving?

MARY: Yeah. I need to take a walk.

CRICK: Whaddya mean, a walk?

MARY: To my mother's.

CRICK: That's a seven-hour walk.

MARY: Yeah. Take care of Blue.

CRICK: What? When will you be back?

MARY: I don't know. Good-bye.

(She leaves, holding her journal.)

CRICK: We were supposed to ride off into the sunset together, Mary. We were.

****

from **Eurydice** (2003)
from Second Movement, Scene 1

CHARACTERS

Eurydice
Big Stone
Little Stone
Loud Stone

[In the first scene of the second movement, a chorus of three stones greets Eurydice to the underworld. Her memory has been erased in the River of Forgetfulness.]

The underworld. There is no set change. Strange watery noises. Drip, drip, drip. The movement to the underworld is marked by the entrance of stones.

THE STONES: We are a chorus of stones.

LITTLE STONE: I'm a little stone.

BIG STONE: I'm a big stone.

LOUD STONE: I'm a loud stone.

THE STONES: We are all three stones.

LITTLE STONE: We live with the dead people in the land of the dead.

BIG STONE: Eurydice was a great musician. Orpheus was his wife.

LOUD STONE: *(Correcting Big Stone.)* Orpheus was a great musician. Eurydice was his wife. She died.

LITTLE STONE: Then he played the saddest music. Even we —

THE STONES: the stones —

LITTLE STONE: cried when we heard it.

(The sound of three drops of water hitting a pond.)

LITTLE STONE: Oh, look, she is coming into the land of the dead now.

BIG STONE: Oh!

LOUD STONE: Oh!

LITTLE STONE: Oh! We might say: "Poor Eurydice" —

LOUD STONE: but stones don't feel bad for dead people.

(The sound of an elevator ding. An elevator door opens. Inside the elevator, it is raining. Eurydice gets rained on inside the elevator. She carries a suitcase and an umbrella. She is dressed in the kind of 1930s suit that women wore when they eloped. She looks bewildered. The sound of an elevator ding. Eurydice steps out of the elevator. The elevator door closes. She walks toward the audience and opens her mouth, trying to speak. There is a great humming noise. She closes her mouth. The humming noise stops. She opens her mouth for the second time, attempting to tell her story to the audience. There is a great humming noise. She closes her mouth — the humming noise stops. She has a tantrum of despair. The Stones, to the audience.)

THE STONES: Eurydice wants to speak to you. But she can't speak your language anymore. She talks in the language of dead people now.

LITTLE STONE: It's a very quiet language.

LOUD STONE: Like if the pores in your face opened up and talked.

BIG STONE: Like potatoes sleeping in the dirt.

(Little Stone and Loud Stone look at Big Stone as though that were a dumb thing to say.)

LITTLE STONE: Pretend that you understand her or she'll be embarrassed.

BIG STONE: Yes — pretend for a moment that you understand the language of stones.

LOUD STONE: Listen to her the way you would listen to your own daughter if she died too young and tried to speak to you across long distances.

(Eurydice shakes out her umbrella. She approaches the audience. This time, she can speak.)

EURYDICE: There was a roar, and a coldness — I think my husband was with me. What was my husband's name?

(Eurydice turns to the Stones.)

EURYDICE: My husband's name? Do you know it?

(The Stones shrug their shoulders.)

EURYDICE: How strange. I don't remember.

It was horrible to see his face when I died. His eyes were two black birds and they flew to me. I said: no — stay where you are — he needs you in order to see! When I got through the cold they made me swim in a river and I forgot his name. I forgot all the names. I know his name starts with my mouth shaped like a ball of twine — Oar — oar. I forget. They took me to a tiny boat. I only just fit inside. I looked at the oars and I wanted to cry. I tried to cry but I just drooled a little. I'll try now.

(She tries to cry but finds that she can't.)

EURYDICE: What happiness it would be to cry.

****

from **The Clean House** (2004)
from Act Two, Scene 10

CHARACTERS

> Lane
> Ana

[In Act Two, Scene 10, Lane makes a house call to treat Ana, the terminally ill cancer patient for whom her husband, Charles, has left her.
At the end of the scene, Charles, who is in Alaska searching for a cure
for Ana's cancer, briefly appears on the stage in a moment of magic
realism.]

On Ana's balcony. Lane listens to Ana's heart with a stethoscope.

LANE: Breathe in. Breathe in again.

(Lane takes off her stethoscope.)

LANE: Are you having any trouble breathing?
ANA: No. But sometimes it hurts when I breathe.
LANE: Where?
ANA: Here.
LANE: Do you have pain when you're at rest?
ANA: Yes.
LANE: Where?
ANA: In my spine.
LANE: Is the pain sharp, or dull?
ANA: Sharp.
LANE: Does it radiate?
ANA: Like light?
LANE: I mean — does it move from one place to another?
ANA: Yes. From here to there.
LANE: How's your appetite?

ANA: Not great. You must hate me.

LANE: Look — I'm being a doctor right now. That's all.

(Lane palpates Ana's spine.)

LANE: Does that hurt?

ANA: It hurts already.

LANE: I can't know anything without doing tests.

ANA: I know.

LANE: And you won't go to the hospital.

ANA: No.

LANE: All right.

ANA: Do you think I'm crazy?

LANE: No.

(A small pause.)

ANA: Well. Can I get you anything to drink? I have some iced tea.

LANE: Sure. Thank you.

(Ana exits. Lane looks out over the balcony at the water. Lane starts to weep. Ana enters with iced tea.)

ANA: Lane?

LANE: Oh God! I'm *not* going to cry in front of you.

ANA: It's OK. You can cry. You must hate me.

LANE: I don't hate you.

ANA: Why are you crying?

LANE: OK! I hate you!

You — glow — with some kind of — thing — I can't *acquire* that — this — thing — sort of — glows off you — like a veil — in reverse — you're like *anyone's* soul mate — because you have that — thing — you have a balcony — I don't have a balcony — Charles looks at you — he glows, too — you're like two glowworms — he never looked at me like that.

ANA: Lane.

LANE: I looked at our wedding pictures to see — maybe — he looked at me that way — back then — and no — he didn't — he looked at me with *admiration* — I didn't know there was another way to be looked at — how could I know — I didn't know his face was capable of *doing that* — the way he looked at you — in my living room.

ANA: I'm sorry.

LANE: No you're not. If you were really sorry, you wouldn't have done it. We do as we please, and then we say we're sorry. But we're not sorry. We're just — uncomfortable — watching other people in pain.

(Ana hands Lane an iced tea.)

LANE: Thank you.

(Lane drinks her iced tea. They both look at the fish in the bowl.)

LANE: What kind of fish is that?

ANA: A fighting fish.

LANE: How old is it?

ANA: Twelve.

LANE: That's old for fish.

ANA: I keep expecting it to die. But it doesn't.

(Lane taps on the bowl. The fish wriggles.)

ANA: How did you and Charles fall in love?

LANE: He didn't tell you?

ANA: No.

LANE: Oh. Well, we were in medical school together. We were anatomy partners. We fell in love over a dead body.

(They look at each other. Lane forgives Ana.)

ANA: Want an apple?

LANE: Sure.

(Ana gives Lane an apple. Lane takes a bite and stops.)

LANE: Did Charles pick this apple?
ANA: I don't know who picked it.

(Lane eats the apple.)

LANE: It's good.

(In the distance, Charles walks across the stage in a heavy parka. He carries a pickax. On the balcony, it is snowing.)

****

CHARACTERS

Jean
Dwight
Gordon

[Jean appropriates Gordon's cell phone after she discovers him dead in a café and takes it upon herself to comfort his relatives and acquaintances. In Part One, Scene 6, after a disastrous dinner with his family, Jean retreats with Gordon's brother, Dwight, to the stationery store at which he works.]

At the stationery store. The supply closet. The light is dim. Jean and Dwight are touching embossed invitations, closing their eyes.

JEAN: Feel this one. Like a leaf.

(Dwight feels it.)

JEAN: This one. Branches. Tablecloths. Wool.

(She passes it to Dwight.)

JEAN: This one is my favorite one, though. I'd like to live in a little house made of this one.

(She passes it to Dwight.)

DWIGHT: A house made of paper.

(Dwight tries to build a little house out of the paper.)

JEAN: Yeah. And this one! Braided hair.

(Dwight touches it.)

DWIGHT: Can I braid your hair?

JEAN: What? OK.

(Dwight stands behind Jean and fumbles with her hair.)

DWIGHT: Am I pulling too hard?

JEAN: No. That's fine. It feels nice.

You know what's funny? I never had a cell phone. I didn't want to always *be there*, you know. Like if your phone is on you're supposed to be there. Sometimes I like to disappear. But it's like — when everyone has their cell phone on, no one is there. It's like we're all disappearing the more we're there. Last week there was this woman in line at the pharmacy and she was like, "Shit, Shit!" on her cell phone and she kept saying, "Shit, fuck, you're shitting me, you're fucking shitting me, no fucking way, bitch, if you're shitting me I'll fucking kill you," you know, that kind of thing, and there were all these old people in line and it was like she didn't care if she told her whole life, the worst part of her life, in front of the people in line. It was like — people who are in line at pharmacies must be strangers. By definition. And I thought that was sad.

But when Gordon's phone rang and rang, after he died, I thought his phone was beautiful, like it was the only thing keeping him alive, like as long as people called him he would be alive. That sounds — a little — I know — but all those molecules, in the air, trying to talk to Gordon — and Gordon — he's in the air too — so maybe they all would meet up there, whizzing around — those bits of air — and voices.

DWIGHT: I wonder how long it will take before no one calls him again and then he will be truly gone.

JEAN: I wonder too. I'll leave his phone on as long as I live. I'll keep recharging it. Just in case someone calls. Maybe an old childhood friend. You never know.

DWIGHT: Did you love my brother?

JEAN: I didn't know him well enough to love him.

DWIGHT: It kind of seems like you do.

JEAN: Were the two of you very close?

DWIGHT: We had our moments. Gordon wasn't always — easy.

JEAN: Tell me a story about him.

DWIGHT: One time Gordon made a character named Mr. Big X and he said: I'll take you to meet Mr. Big X! I was really excited to meet Mr. Big X. But in order to meet him, Gordon wrapped me up in a blanket and pushed me down the stairs.

JEAN: You have any nice stories about Gordon?

DWIGHT: Yeah. They're just harder to remember, you know. No imprint. Like — one time we had dinner — Gordon was nice to me — and — what kind of story is that . . .

JEAN: You crying?

DWIGHT: I'm OK.

JEAN: How's that braid coming?

DWIGHT: It's pretty good. I've never done a braid before.

(Jean reaches up and feels the braid.)

JEAN: It's good. Only you did two parts, not three.

DWIGHT: Huh?

JEAN: Usually a braid has three parts. Two parts is more like a twist. But that's fine. I bet it's pretty from the back.

DWIGHT: It does look pretty.

Here — let me show you —

(He tries to show her the twist. Their faces are close to each other, in the dark, in the back of the stationery store. Jean and Dwight kiss. Gordon's cell phone rings.)

DWIGHT: Don't answer that.

JEAN: It could be —

DWIGHT: Don't get it. It'll take a message, OK?

JEAN: But I can't get Gordon's messages — I don't have his password! I'll never know who called —

DWIGHT: Their number — on the in-coming calls — will be saved.
OK?
JEAN: OK.

(The phone rings. They kiss. Embossed stationery moves through the air slowly, like a snow parade. Lanterns made of embossed paper, houses made of embossed paper, light falling on paper, falling on Jean and Dwight, who are also falling.)

(Gordon walks onstage. He opens his mouth, as if to speak to the audience. Blackout.)

INTERMISSION

****

from **Passion Play, a cycle in three parts** (2007)
from Part One, Scenes 8 and 9

CHARACTERS

Pontius
Mary 1
John

[Each part of *Passion Play* is set during a different historical period: Elizabethan England, Nazi Germany, and America from the Vietnam War through the Reagan era. In each part, a group of actors stages the biblical Passion, and the extent to which each character merges with or diverges from his or her biblical role is examined. In Part One, Pontius plays Pontius Pilate, his cousin John plays Jesus, and Mary 1 plays the Virgin Mary. Pontius is a wretched fish gutter, John a saintly fisherman, and Mary 1, definitely not a virgin. In the following excerpt, Mary 1 ventures out at night in search of male companionship.]

SCENE 8: NIGHT

Pontius sits on a stoop, cleaning his shoes with a knife.

PONTIUS: Last night the moon threw its head back, laughing at me — a white wedge — a laughing pitchfork — and tonight the moon sank down on his haunches — his face turned full at me — he looked bewildered and afraid. Had the fat white face of a dunce. You think I'm a bloody fool to speak of the moon, but who else will be a witness to my grief?

The doctor who birthed me, see, he didn't sew up my belly properly. Most people have got some skin between their guts and the air of the world, not me, not me. You can stick your finger way into my belly button, and when you pull it out it smells like gangrene, like fish.

I gut the fish. My cousin — he catches 'em. He don't have to see their innards. He don't have to talk to dead fish all day. He can talk to the sea. Me — I close my nose and I smell the stench of dead fish. I close my eyes and see dead fish coming at me in a parade.

He closes his eyes and huge puppet fish walk toward him as if in a parade. They surround him and undress him. They leave to the beating of drums. He turns to the audience. He blinks. The sound of the sea gurgles.

SCENE 9: NIGHT

Mary 1 kneels by her bed.

MARY 1: Hail Mary, full of grace . . .

(To the audience.)

MARY 1: I hate to sleep alone. My feet get cold. I put socks on and then my feet get hot so I take them off under the blankets but then my feet get cold again in the night.

(Putting her socks on.)

MARY 1: It's unnatural, cold and unnatural, this solitary sleeping. The sheep sleep together, all woolly and warm. I get too lonesome to sleep alone. I slept with my parents til I got too old. One time they locked me out — I could hear why — strange sounds coming from the bed. When I got old enough I found men to sleep with — men with hair on their legs and bellies to keep me warm at night. I go out walking sometimes to find them.

(She climbs down a rope and out of her window.)

MARY 1: I've never been with child. Don't know why. Better not to ask God.

(John the Fisherman out walking in a shaft of light.)

JOHN: Sometimes — tonight — a feeling of grace comes and I feel peaceful and easy and ready to die but still aware of the moon's beauty, like silver fish scales shedding. Skin covers the world — luminous moon skin — and I must step softly and slowly on it — the cobbled streets have fish skin, the trees have human skin — and it is not fearsome, only slow and lovely and soft, but I must be careful not to prick you and make you bleed.

MARY 1: *(Walking toward him, carrying a jar.)* Good evening.

JOHN: Good evening, Mary. What brings you into the night air by yourself?

MARY 1: Uuum . . . My mother — she's sick — doctor told me to trap the night air in a jar and bring it back to her.

JOHN: May I help?

(Mary looks down, embarrassed.)

MARY 1: Umm —

JOHN: I'd do anything to help you and your good mother, Mary.

MARY 1: Could you climb up that tree, John, and trap that particular spot of air?

(She hands him a jar and he climbs an abstracted version of a wagon.)

JOHN: This spot?

(She scrutinizes him from behind.)

MARY 1: Perhaps a bit higher
        And up. Yes, that bit there.

JOHN: *(Handing her the jar.)* I hope this will do, Mary.

(She smiles at him.)

JOHN: Your mother . . . is she very sick?

MARY 1: My mother? . . . oh yes . . . her belly . . . she swallowed something . . .

JOHN: I'm sorry, Mary. You know I would drink your sorrow if I could.

(John escorts Mary 1 offstage.)

****

from **Passion Play, a cycle in three parts** (2007)
from Part Three, Scene 9

CHARACTERS

Queen Elizabeth
Ronald Reagan
P
Violet
A Soldier

[Each part of *Passion Play* is set during a different historical period: Elizabethan England, Nazi Germany, and America from the Vietnam War through the Reagan era. In each part, a group of actors stages the biblical Passion. The extent to which each character merges or diverges with his or her biblical part is played out. In Part Three, Scene 9, the veteran known simply as P, who plays Pontius Pilate in the Passion, appeals to President Reagan for absolution for violence committed against civilians in the Vietnam War. Queen Elizabeth, who plays a larger role in the first part, asynchronously escorts Reagan onto the stage. Violet is P's young daughter. P has previously driven a nail through his hand during a fit of rage at a rehearsal.]

Ronald Reagan escorted by Queen Elizabeth, played by another actor. They walk behind a coffin, draped with an American flag. Violet scatters petals before them. The coffin is laid down. It is the tomb of the unknown soldier. A subtitle reads: 1984. Dedication ceremony, Vietnam War Memorial. Queen Elizabeth departs. A member of the ensemble, dressed as a soldier, guarding the tomb. P watching, his hand crushed at his side.

REAGAN: The Unknown Soldier who is returned to us today and whom we lay to rest is symbolic of all our missing sons. Thank you dear son, may God cradle you in his loving arms.

I was once an actor, you know. People say I wear a little rouge on my cheeks. It's not true. When I am laid to rest, my cheeks will be rosy still.

(He places a wreath on the grave. A military salute.)

REAGAN: I never did serve in the military. But I feel as though I did.

(Reagan salutes P. P salutes Reagan.)

P: You're good at that.

REAGAN: I made training films for soldiers, during the war. I learned to salute. It was one of the happiest times of my life.

(Reagan salutes P. P salutes Reagan.)

P: That was a good speech. Did you write it?

(Reagan smiles.)

REAGAN: Bob Hope once asked me what it's like being President. I said "it's not a lot different than being an actor, except I get to write the script."

(He chuckles.)

REAGAN: No, I didn't write this speech, son, but I did make some little changes. Sometimes the writers don't know where the applause lines ought to be. I was supposed to end with: "fighting for human dignity."

I saw that the applause line oughta be: "Thank you, dear son. May God cradle you in His loving arms." So I changed it. The press thought: oh, the old bumbler, he's forgotten his lines again. Well, the joke's on them.

What happened to your hand?

P: I crucified Pontius Pilate. Why not crucify the bad guy for once. You know?

REAGAN: Not really.

Why have you come to see me, son?

P: I wanted to ask: if a man is following orders, and he does something bad, does he have to wash his own hands, or does the leader wash his hands?

REAGAN: It seems to me you need to see a priest. But I will wash your hands, if you'd like me to.

(P nods.)

REAGAN: Let's see, there must be some water in Washington, D.C. Some water!

(A soldier goes to get a glass of water for Reagan.)

REAGAN: Sure is hot. I was a lifeguard on the Rock River, you know. Saved 77 lives on the Rock River. If the tide is too much for you, I will save you.

(The soldier returns with the water and gives it to Reagan.)

REAGAN: *(To P.)* Kneel down.

(P does.)

REAGAN: I wash your hands of the sins you committed. In the name of the Father, the Son, and the Holy —

P: Please, no God stuff.

REAGAN: How else will you wash away your sins if not with the language of God?

P: Just the water.

REAGAN: The water will do nothing without the language of God.

P: Then don't wash me.

REAGAN: All right.

Boy is it hot.

(Reagan drinks the water himself.)

REAGAN: Ah! Delicious. Good old American tap water.

   Son, I think it's time for you to go home.

   Where's home?

P: All over.

REAGAN: Everyone is from somewhere.

P: I used to be from South Dakota.

REAGAN: Well, it's your lucky day. I'm going to campaign there tomorrow. My campaign manager brought me the ratings. He said, what can we do to get those ratings up? Get shot again, I said. It was a joke!

   So we can mosey on over to South Dakota together. I'll be riding my horse. Don't you see it?

(P shakes his head.)

REAGAN: Where's my hat?

(Someone throws him a cowboy hat. He waves his hat.)

REAGAN: So long!

(He exits.)

****

from **In the Next Room (or the vibrator play)** (2009)

from Act Two, Scene 2

CHARACTERS

Mrs. Givings
Elizabeth
Leo

[The play is set in the 1880s. In this excerpt from Act Two, Scene 2, Mrs. Givings bids farewell in turn to Elizabeth and Leo. Elizabeth, who has lost her own infant child, has been employed to wet nurse the Givings' baby. Mrs. Givings is white; Elizabeth is black. Leo enters after Elizabeth's departure. Disenchanted with her marriage, Mrs. Givings has fallen for the artist, who is being treated by her husband for male hysteria. He gently rejects her as he departs for Paris.]

ELIZABETH: I wanted to say good-bye to Lotty.

MRS. GIVINGS: Of course. She is in the nursery.

ELIZABETH: Thank you. I have grown fond of her.

MRS. GIVINGS: Yes. She is fat and happy, all thanks to you, Elizabeth. I never thanked you because I was jealous. I can be a small woman, small indeed. What on earth will we do without you?

ELIZABETH: She is almost ready to have cow's milk. Or a little bit of rice pudding.

MRS. GIVINGS: I was not thinking of the food. Well. She is in the nursery. Elizabeth — how old was your Henry Douglas when he died?

ELIZABETH: Twelve weeks.

MRS. GIVINGS: What did he die of?

ELIZABETH: Cholera.

MRS. GIVINGS: I am sorry.

ELIZABETH: Thank you.

MRS. GIVINGS: And how do you go on after?

ELIZABETH: My mother told me to pray each day since I was a little girl, to pray that you borrow everything, everyone you love, from God. That way you aren't too sad when you have to repay the loan and give your son, or your mother, or your husband, back to God. I prayed Jesus, let me be humble in case I have to give your gift back to you. I borrowed my child, I borrowed my husband, I borrowed my own life from you, God. But he felt like *mine* not like God's he felt like mine more *mine* than anything.

God must have this huge horrible cabinet — all the babies who get returned — and all those babies inside, they're all crying even with God, with God Himself to rock them to sleep, still they want their mothers. So when I started to feel something for this baby, for your baby, I thought no, everything that's worth having is borrowed, borrowed, gone.

When I first met her all I could think was: she is alive and Henry is not. I had all this milk — I wished it would dry up. Just get through the year, I thought. Your milk will dry up and you will forget. The more healthy your baby got, the more dead my baby became. I thought of her like a tick. I thought — fill her up and then pop! You will see the blood of my Henry underneath. But she seemed so grateful for the milk. Sometimes I hated her for it. But she would look at me, she would give me this look — I do not know what to call it if it is not called love. I hope that every day you keep her — you keep her close to you — and you remember the blood that her milk was made from.

MRS. GIVINGS: I will.

(Mrs. Givings holds Elizabeth's hands in hers. It is the first and only time they have touched — they have passed the baby between them without ever touching. Elizabeth nods and exits, to the nursery. Mrs. Givings, alone.

She goes to the operating theater. She hesitates. The doorbell rings. It is Leo.)

MRS. GIVINGS: You have made quite a mess of things for Elizabeth.

LEO: I know. I'm sorry. I've come to say good-bye. I'm moving to Paris.

MRS. GIVINGS: When?

LEO: Tomorrow.

MRS. GIVINGS: That's not possible. You're leaving me? That is to say — you're leaving?

LEO: Yes.

MRS. GIVINGS: Take me with you.

LEO: Are you out of your mind?

MRS. GIVINGS: You are surprised? It was you who seduced me!

LEO: What?

MRS. GIVINGS: All that talk of women, two thirds done, that was me, you were talking of me, were you not?

LEO: I was talking of paintings. I —

MRS. GIVINGS: No one has ever spoken to me of those things before. Of beauty — of prostitutes, of — my God, of *Italy*. How could I have misunderstood your intentions? I'm in love with you.

LEO: Oh, dear Catherine I'm afraid I cannot love you. If there is any type to whom I am attracted — it veers toward women with doe eyes. And your eyes are more — they are more — thin — the light bounces off them rather than into them. And I cannot see your soul hovering here, where I would like to, two inches away. Your soul is locked somewhere inside your body, so I cannot see it. Another man could perhaps bring your soul outside your eyes but it's not me, I'm afraid. I do care for you though.

MRS. GIVINGS: Try. Try to bring my soul out — to here. If you look into my eyes — see — I will try. See!

(He does not.)

MRS. GIVINGS: Are you bringing another woman with you?

LEO: No — I'm going alone.

       Don't you see? It is Elizabeth who I love.

MRS. GIVINGS: Elizabeth?

LEO: Yes. And she doesn't care for me, not at all, I told her of my affections on our walk and she slapped me. And then her mother slapped her. There was quite a lot of slapping. No — I will go to Paris alone. I am married to my solitude.

MRS. GIVINGS: I can be your solitude. I'll be quiet as a mouse. I understand solitude, I am very lonely.

LEO: I do not understand your loneliness, Mrs. Givings. You have a child, a husband — *a home!*

MRS. GIVINGS: Yes. I am very ungrateful. I am sure that God will punish me.

(She tries to embrace him.)

LEO: No. You do not love me. You only think you do. You love your husband. He is a good man.

(He kisses her hands.)

LEO: Good-bye, now. Come visit me in France. I promise you — you'll love the paintings.

MRS. GIVINGS: Elizabeth is in the nursery. If you wish to say good-bye to her.

LEO: I can't bear to see her. Just give her this, won't you?

(Leo kisses Mrs. Givings on the cheek. He leaves.)

****

THE READING ROOM

YOUNG ACTORS AND THEIR TEACHERS

Reid, Kerry. "Truth on a Slant." *Performlnk Online*, May 26, 2006.
http://www.performink.com/Archives/stagepersonae/2006/STAGE
PERSONAE_SarahRuhl.htm

STUDENTS, SCHOLARS, PROFESSORS

Al-Shamma, James. *Sarah Ruhl* (working title). Jefferson, N.C.: McFar-
land, forthcoming.

THEATERS, PRODUCERS

Piven Theatre Workshop. www.piventheatre.org.

ACTORS, DIRECTORS, THEATER PROFESSIONALS

Greene, Alexis, ed. "An Interview with Sarah Ruhl." *Women Writing Plays:
Three Decades of The Susan Smith Blackburn Prize*. Louann Atkins
Temple Women & Culture Series. Austin: University of Texas Press,
2006. 228–233.

————. "Joking Aside: A Conversation about Comedy with Christopher
Durang, Gina Gionfriddo, Sarah Ruhl, and Wendy Wasserstein." *Women
Writing Plays: Three Decades of The Susan Smith Blackburn Prize*.
Louann Atkins Temple Women & Culture Series. Austin: University of
Texas Press, 2006. 181–190.

Gurewitsch, Matthew. "Wild Woman." *Smithsonian,* fall 2007.

Hansen, Liane, host. "A Promising Playwright's Summer Authors." *Week-
end Edition Sunday,* National Public Radio. July 15, 2007.
www.npr.org/templates/story/story.php?storyId=11979557.

This extensive bibliography lists books about the playwright according to whom the books might be of interest. If you would
like to research further something that interests you in the text, lists of references, sources cited, and editions used in this
book are found in this section.

──────. "What Are Your Summer Reads?" *NPR Special Series*, National Public Radio. August 26, 2007. www.npr.org/templates/story/story.php?storyId=475921.

Kaplan, Lila Rose. "In Dialogue: Inhabiting *The Clean House* with Sarah Ruhl." *The Brooklyn Rail*, October 2004. www.thebrooklynrail.org.

Lahr, John. "Gods and Dolls: Sarah Ruhl Reimagines the Orpheus Myth." *The New Yorker*, July 2, 2007.

Renner, Pamela. "Spiritual Cleanliness: An Interview with the Playwright." *American Theatre* 21, no. 9 (November 2004): 50.

Shteir, Rachel. "Home Fires." *Chicago Magazine*, May 2006. www.chicagomag.com/Chicago-Magazine/May-2006/Home-Fires.

Stamberg, Susan, host. "Paula Vogel: Remembering Through Language." *Morning Edition*, National Public Radio. December 7, 2004. www.npr.org/templates/story/story.php?storyId=4205954.

──────. "Scenes I Wish I'd Written." *NPR Special Series*, National Public Radio. December 28, 2004. www.npr.org/templates/story/story.php?storyId=4160995.

EDITIONS OF RUHL'S WORKS USED FOR THIS BOOK

Ruhl, Sarah. *"The Lady with the Lap Dog" and "Anna Around the Neck": Two Stories by Anton Chekhov*. Unpublished script, 2000.

──────. *Virtual Meditation #1*. Unpublished script, 2002.

──────. *Dog Play*. Unpublished script, 2002.

──────. *Orlando*. Unpublished script, 2003.

──────. *The Clean House and Other Plays*. New York: Theatre Communications Group, 2006.

──────. *Demeter in the City*. Unpublished script, 2006.

──────. *Passion Play, A Cycle in Three Parts*. Unpublished script, 2007.

──────. *Dead Man's Cell Phone*. New York: Theatre Communications Group, 2008.

──────. *Snowless*. Unpublished script, 2008.

SOURCES CITED IN THIS BOOK

Berry, Dawn Bradley. *The Domestic Violence Sourcebook: Everything You Need to Know*. Los Angeles: NTC Contemporary, 1998.

Butler, Judith. *Gender Trouble: Feminism and the Subversion of Identity*. New York: Routledge, 1999.

Calvino, Italo. *Six Memos for the Next Millennium*. Cambridge, Mass.: Harvard University Press, 1988.

Capra, Frank, dir. *It's a Wonderful Life*. With James Stewart and Donna Reed. Los Angeles: RKO Pictures, 1946.

"A Conversation with Sarah Ruhl and Blair Brown." *Lincoln Center Theater*, November 15, 2006. www.lctstudentix.org/content/platform/Clean HousePlatform.pdf.

Creamer, Tom. "Queen, Fuehrer, President: Politics, Passion and Play." *Onstage* (Goodman Theatre) 23, no. 1 (September–December 2007): 6–9.

Fausto-Sterling, Anne. *Sexing the Body: Gender Politics and the Construction of Sexuality*. New York: Basic Books, 2000.

Gianopulos, Peter. "The Passion of Sarah Ruhl." *North Shore Magazine*, September 2007. www.northshoremag.com.

Goodman, Lawrence. "Playwright Laureate of Grief." *Brown Alumni Magazine*, March/April 2007. www.brownalumnimagazine.com/content/view/288/40.

Gray, Channing. "Sarah Ruhl's *Melancholy Play* Opens at Leeds Theatre." *Providence (RI) Journal*, November 8, 2007. www.projo.com/theater/content/wk-melancholyplay_11-08-07_TF7OGIT_v12.15d4988.html.

Guare, John. *Bosoms and Neglect*. New York: Dramatists Play Service, 1980.

Helmetag, Charles H. "Mother Courage and Her American Cousins in *The Skin of Our Teeth*." *Modern Language Studies* 8, no. 3 (Autumn 1978): 65–69.

Kennedy, Louise. "A Season of Grief." *Boston Globe*, December 24, 2006, first ed.: N1. www.boston.com/ae/theater_arts/articles/2006/12/24/a_season_of_grief/.

Kushner, Tony. *Angels in America: A Gay Fantasia on National Themes. Part One: Millennium Approaches*. New York: Theatre Communications Group, 1993.

———. *Angels in America: A Gay Fantasia on National Themes. Part Two: Perestroika*. Rev. version. New York: Theatre Communications Group, 1996.

Lahr, John. "Surreal Life: The Plays of Sarah Ruhl." A Critic at Large. *The New Yorker*, March 17, 2008. www.newyorker.com/arts/critics/atlarge/2008/03/17/080317crat_atlarge_lahr.

Palmer, Tanya. "A Passion for Theater: Interview with Sarah Ruhl." *Onstage* (Goodman Theatre) 23, no. 1 (September–December 2007): 2–5.

———. "Directing *Passion Play*: An Interview with Mark Wing-Davey." *Onstage* (Goodman Theatre) 23, no. 1 (September–December 2007): 10–12.

Polikoff, Joan, Nader Nazmi, and Sarah Ruhl. *Troika VI: Swimming Toward Birth; Across Roses; Death in Another Country.* Winnetka, Ill.: Thorntree Press, 1995.

Pressley, Nelson. "The Golden Ruhl: Playwright Has a Midas Touch." *Washington Post,* final ed.: N01. Sunday Arts. September 4, 2005. www.washingtonpost.com/wp-dyn/content/article/2005/09/02/AR2005090200565.html.

"Production Notebook: Sarah Ruhl's *Eurydice* at Yale Repertory Theatre." *American Theatre* 23, no. 10 (December 2006): 36–37.

Reid, Kerry. "Truth on a Slant." *PerformInk Online,* May 26, 2006. http://www.performink.com/Archives/stagepersonae/2006/STAGE PERSONAE_SarahRuhl.htm

Royce, Graydon. "OnStage: 'House' Proud." *Minneapolis-St. Paul Star Tribune,* October 18, 2007. www.startribune.com/onstage.

Ruhl, Sarah. "Six Small Thoughts on Fornes, the Problem of Intention, and Willfulness." *Theatre Topics* 11, no. 2 (September 2001): 187–204.

Savran, David. *In Their Own Words: Contemporary American Playwrights.* New York: Theatre Communications Group, 1988.

Smith, Dinitia. "Playwright's Subjects: Greek Myths to Vibrators." *New York Times,* October 14, 2006: B7. www.nytimes.com/2006/10/14/theater/14ruhl.html?_r=1.

Stamberg, Susan, host. "Playwright Sarah Ruhl Entertains with Big Ideas." *Morning Edition,* National Public Radio. October 21, 2005. www.npr.org/templates/story/story.php?storyId=4967202.

Svitch, Caridad. "In Conversation with Sarah Ruhl." *The Dramatist* 4, no. 3 (2002): 36–39.

Virtual Meditation #1. Carnegie Mellon University Entertainment Technology Center. www.etc.cmu.edu/projects/atl/index.htm.

Vogel, Paula. "Sarah Ruhl." *Bomb* 99 (Spring 2007): 54–59. www.bomb site.com/issues/99/articles/2902.

Weber, Carl. "I Always Go Back to Brecht." *Tony Kushner in Conversation.* Robert Vorlicky, ed. Ann Arbor: University of Michigan Press, 1998. 105–24.

Weckwerth, Wendy. "More Invisible Terrains: Sarah Ruhl, Interviewed by Wendy Weckwerth." *Theater* 34, no. 2 (2004): 28–35.

Wilder, Thornton. *Three Plays: Our Town, The Skin of Our Teeth, The Matchmaker.* New York: Bantam, 1957.

————. *The Collected Short Plays of Thornton Wilder.* Vol. I. Donald Gallup and A. Tappan Wilder, eds. New York: Theatre Communications Group, 1997.

Wren, Celia. "The Golden Ruhl." *American Theatre* 22, no. 8 (October 2005).

Awards

"And the winner is . . . "

Passion Play, The Fourth Freedom Forum Playwriting Award from
   The Kennedy Center, 2000

Whiting Writers' Award, 2003

Helen Merrill Emerging Playwrights Award, 2003

The Clean House, Susan Smith Blackburn Prize, 2004

The Clean House, Pulitzer Prize Finalist, 2005

The Clean House, Harold and Mimi Steinberg/American Theatre
   Critics Association New Play Citation, 2005

Passion Play, a cycle, Helen Hayes Awards nomination for best new
   play, 2006

MacArthur Fellowship ("Genius" Grant), 2006

Dead Man's Cell Phone, Harold and Mimi Steinberg/American Theatre
   Critics Association New Play Citation, 2008

Dead Man's Cell Phone, Helen Hayes Award for best new play, 2008

	PULITZER PRIZE	TONY AWARD	NY DRAMA CRITICS CIRCLE AWARD		
			Best American	Best Foreign	Best Play
1998	Paula Vogel *How I Learned to Drive*	Yasmina Reza *Art*	Tina Howe *Pride's Crossing*	No Award	Yasmina Reza *Art*
1999	Margaret Edson *Wit*	Warren Leight *Side Man*	No Award	Patrick Marber *Closer*	Margaret Edson *Wit*
2000	Donald Margulies *Dinner with Friends*	Michael Frayn *Copenhagen*	No Award	Michael Frayn *Copenhagen*	August Wilson *Jitney*
2001	David Auburn *Proof*	David Auburn *Proof*	David Auburn *Proof*	No Award	Tom Stoppard *The Invention of Love*

This awards chart is provided for reference so you can see who was winning the major writing awards during the writing career of the playwright.

	PULITZER PRIZE	TONY AWARD	NY DRAMA CRITICS CIRCLE AWARD		
			Best American	Best Foreign	Best Play
2002	Suzan-Lori Parks *Topdog/Underdog*	Edward Albee *The Goat: or, Who Is Sylvia?*	Edward Albee *The Goat: or, Who Is Sylvia?*		
2003	Nilo Cruz *Anna in the Tropics*	Richard Greenburg *Take Me Out*	No Award	Alan Bennett *Talking Heads*	Richard Greenburg *Take Me Out*
2004	Doug Wright *I Am My Own Wife*	Doug Wright *I Am My Own Wife*	Lynn Nottage *Intimate Apparel*		
2005	John Patrick Shanley *Doubt, a Parable*	John Patrick Shanley *Doubt, a Parable*	No Award	Martin McDonagh *The Pillowman*	John Patrick Shanley *Doubt, a Parable*
2006	No Award	Alan Bennet *The History Boys*	Alan Bennett *The History Boys*		
2007	David Lindsay-Abaire *Rabbit Hole*	Tom Stoppard *The Coast of Utopia*	August Wilson *Radio Gulf*	No Award	Tom Stoppard *The Coast of Utopia*
2008	Tracy Letts *August: Osage County*	Tracy Letts *August: Osage County*	Tracy Letts *August: Osage County*		

INDEX

The entries in the index include highlights from the main In an Hour essay portion of the book.

AUTHOR BIOGRAPHY

James Al-Shamma received his B.F.A. in acting and M.A. and Ph.D. in dramatic art from the University of California, Santa Barbara. He teaches theater history, dramatic literature and criticism, and script-writing at Belmont University in Nashville, Tennessee. He is also a director and actor.

ACKNOWLEDGMENTS

Thanks to Simon Williams and Judith Olauson, and a special thanks to William Davies King. Many thanks to the playwright herself for generously sharing unpublished scripts.

NOTE FROM THE PUBLISHER

We thank Theatre Communications Group, Sarah Ruhl, and her agent Bruce Ostler, whose enlightened permissions policies reflect an understanding that copyright law is intended to both protect the rights of creators of intellectual property as well as to encourage its use for the public good.

Know the playwright, love the play.

Open a new door to theater study, performance, and audience satisfaction with these Playwrights In an Hour titles.

ANCIENT GREEK

Aeschylus   Aristophanes   Euripides   Sophocles

RENAISSANCE

William Shakespeare

MODERN

Anton Chekhov   Noël Coward   Lorraine Hansberry
Henrik Ibsen   Arthur Miller   Molière   Eugene O'Neill
Arthur Schnitzler   George Bernard Shaw   August Strindberg
Frank Wedekind   Oscar Wilde   Thornton Wilder
Tennessee Williams

CONTEMPORARY

Edward Albee   Alan Ayckbourn   Samuel Beckett
Theresa Rebeck   Sarah Ruhl   Sam Shepard   Tom Stoppard
August Wilson

To purchase or for more information
visit our web site inanhourbooks.com